WILLIAM BROWNING

SHOULDA BEEN DEAD:
A LIFE
WELL LIVED

AuthorHouse™
1663 Liberty Drive
Bloomington, IN 47403
www.authorhouse.com
Phone: 833-262-8899

Because of the dynamic nature of the Internet, any web addresses or links contained in this book may have changed since publication and may no longer be valid. The views expressed in this work are solely those of the author and do not necessarily reflect the views of the publisher, and the publisher hereby disclaims any responsibility for them.

Any people depicted in stock imagery provided by Getty Images are models, and such images are being used for illustrative purposes only. Certain stock imagery © Getty Images.

This book is printed on acid-free paper.

ISBN: 979-8-8230-2434-1 (sc)
ISBN: 979-8-8230-2442-6 (hc)
ISBN: 979-8-8230-2435-8 (e)

Library of Congress Control Number: 2024906251

Print information available on the last page.

Published by AuthorHouse 05/06/2024

authorHOUSE®

FOREWORD

My friend Marty Engler wrote a book called *Foxhunt 24* about his adventures in Europe during World War II. That inspired me to jot down some of my flying adventures and led to an enjoyable journey for me. So many cherished memories, in addition to some others, led me to select the title for this book!

I hope my treasured friend, George Fenzl, will forgive me for sharing our foibles during the college years and in the Navy. In addition to being my partner in lots of fun during the early years, he was also a career Naval aviator and war hero.

Special thanks to my friend Kate Engler, the daughter of my flying partner and friend, Marty. Over many taco salads and good Chardonnay at our favorite Mexican restaurant, we converted a rough sketch into an organized story. She also helped me with editing and all the other steps throughout the publishing process. My daughter, Suzie Lincoln, also provided invaluable editing, support, and suggestions.

This book is dedicated to my wife, Sadako, along with all my family and friends who, with their love and support, made mine *A Life Well Lived*, indeed.

CONTENTS

BENNINGTON

The Bennington Battle Monument is an imposing 306-foot-high obelisk commemorating the Battle of Bennington, which marked the turning point of the American Revolution. A large area of the surrounding countryside can be viewed from the observation platform near the top. The small road which circles the monument also provides access for the four or five luxurious homes surrounding the monument.

Bennington Monument.

I was fortunate to be born in Vermont, with good memories of Bennington. Our first home was on Washington Avenue. It was a small white house; I don't remember the interior. Lee Warner, who lived across the street was head of the Cushman Furniture Company in North Bennington. We still have a footstool made by Cushman, and much of our dining furniture was from there at one time. Lee was also a photographer; he taught me how to develop black and white film and was generous in letting a little kid like me use his darkroom.

As my dad's medical practice grew, we moved to a bigger house on Union Street, which served as a medical office as well. We lived there until 7th or 8th grade, when we moved to the country on Morgan Street Extension.

Our 17-room house on Union Street home was palatial for Bennington, with a cupola on the front roof above the second story. We rented it for $68 per month! Dad was big on Christmas decorations, and one year he got a large cardboard Santa from the drug store candy display, and mounted it on the top of the cupola, illuminated with a spotlight.

There was a piano room at the very front of the house, a living room behind that, a formal dining room behind that, and a large kitchen with a pantry. On the second floor my room had a secret panel into the guest room, in the event of fire. My sister had a room down the hall toward the master bedroom, at the front of the house, which seemed very large and luxurious to a child my age. Behind the kitchen was a hall to the maid's quarters – we had maids at various times during those years. One maid was very starched and proper; I don't remember her smiling. Another was a woman called Effie. She was just the opposite and hard of hearing. She wore a gray uniform, but her long sleeved underwear stuck out below the sleeves and never looked very clean. If you asked her for something from the kitchen, the answer usually was a very loud, "Whadja want?" I don't think she stayed long.

Dad arranged a playroom for me off the back hall, behind which was a tool room with a door out to the carriage barn. That long house reminded me of a passenger train! The back part of the house was not heated except by a stove in the middle of the playroom, which also may have served as a workshop. One year Dad was constructing a large Lionel Train layout as a Christmas surprise for me. I ventured back to that room when I heard a train whistle, and he was very upset at the intrusion.

The long driveway ran from the street to the carriage barn and then made a circle in the backyard with a garden and a birdbath in the middle. Dad had a rock garden behind the garage and took great pride in that. He had a waterfall and many specimen plants, some of which were desert plants and succulents, despite the Vermont weather.

The spacious side yard went up a steep back hill almost to the next street. My friends and I used to go sledding from the top down into the side yard, zipping all the way to the street in front. One winter my dad built a four-sided berm in the side yard and he stood outside on long cold nights with the garden hose making a skating rink. I wasn't a very good skater but enjoyed it with many kids from the neighborhood. My mother used to serve hot chocolate when we were skating in the cold.

During the summer that yard was also a pleasant place for picnic lunches. When we were kindergarten age, a little girl named Sally, a dentist's daughter who used to live near us at the earlier home, would be dropped off for play visits. My mother would make "tea" for us at a child-sized outdoor table. Sally announced to my mother, "When I'm grown up, I'm going to live here." My mother replied, "But this is my house, dear." My young friend then responded, "Oh, you'll be dead by then!"

During the long summers some boys from the neighborhood used to play football in the side yard. The yard was bordered by peonies, and I remember being hired by my dad to weed them for 5 cents an hour.

The Doctor

There was a maple tree for climbing, and I broke my elbow falling out of it. Dad set it under chloroform anesthesia in the O.R., and I remember a dream of being in a large glass sphere, with an octopus trying to grab my painful arm. Dad had an ingenious idea of immobilizing the fracture with dual steel turnbuckle splints allowing the elbow to be moved gradually through a range of motion while it was healing. All the other kids wanted that treatment instead of a plaster cast, since it allowed swimming in the splint during that summer.

Dad's medical office was in our house for several years. Our phone number was only 3 digits, requiring an operator to route the call to the office or the home. Our phone number, 696, was for both work and residence. The home got one ring at 696R and the office, 696W, got two rings. When we went to four digits, the new number, 4806, was a big jump in sophistication!

After Dad moved to the office on Main Street with a large comfortable waiting room and two exam rooms, he shared space with another doctor.

Dad's nurse Leona was a wonderful lady, a devout Catholic, and a spinster who couldn't marry her boyfriend because he was a divorced Protestant. Like many excellent nurses, she anchored the office and kept things going smoothly. One birthday she gave me a 33-rpm record player and a copy of Tchaikovsky's First Symphony; I'm sure I wore out that record. She also taught me to dance in our living room, for which I was very grateful when I got to high school. Midnight Mass at the big Catholic Church was always inspiring and despite my Episcopal upbringing, I would always go to Christmas Midnight Mass at St. Francis with her. She was a moral and spiritual inspiration.

Years later the Okinawan relatives gave me the last word in Christmas presents, a necktie with a tiny module that played "Jingle Bells" when pressed. I wore that tie to the midnight Candlelight service. In that sacred moment when everyone had a candle, the lights were out, and "Silent Night" was being sung softly while kneeling in prayer, I dozed off and leaned against the pew in front of me, at which point "Jingle Bells" echoed throughout the church!

Dad delivered 5000 babies in Bennington during his practice, about half the town population. He let me observe office procedures (with the patient's consent) or help with sharpening and sterilizing hypodermic needles, since reuse was the norm at that time. They certainly weren't as painless as the current aluminum one-use variety!

The Putnam Memorial Hospital served our town well and Dad sometimes took me with him when he made rounds. The nurses had to make chart entries in ink, blue for favorable and red for unfavorable. They were kind enough not to inform my dad that I was mixing the inks in the inkwells to get a prettier color!

Ladies' clubs were quite popular, and my mother Florence belonged to the Bridge Club and the Garden Club, with regular luncheon meetings of both. She loved flowers and gardening and spent a lot of time tending her garden. As a youngster, I got the impression the bridge clubs could more readily be called gossip clubs. The host vied to prepare the best dessert or snacks at these events as well. Prior to the days of the internet, those clubs were a good way to swap knowledge about garden care among other things.

Mom and Dad always had two convertible cars, Chevrolets first and then Pontiacs. Later, Dad had a '52 Buick Roadmaster convertible which I really wanted after finishing college. However, as he had always done, he traded it in for a new car and he shocked us by getting a pink and black Pontiac sedan.

Dad was in big trouble when he sold Mom's '55 T-bird, replacing it with a mediocre Chevy sedan. After he traded in his Buick Roadmaster, I had to buy it back from Bill Edington's Chevrolet. It served me well. I drove it to Florida during flight training, then to San Diego, and eventually it went to Oakland, for shipment to its final years in Okinawa, where it might still be. (The story of the San Diego to Oakland trip comes later.)

Horses

Before we moved to the country, the doctor who shared the office with my dad gave me a horse. I never did find out what kind of favor led to that large gift, but I suspect it may have had something to do with an affair with the other doctor's nurse, and perhaps Dad had something to do with salvaging things with his wife.

Dad built a stall for the horse, Firecracker. Despite his name, he was fairly cooperative. Dad also bought an old-fashioned Santa Claus sleigh, and we harnessed up the horse and went for short dashes in the snow-covered streets.

It was fortunate that we soon moved out to the country since Firecracker was not entirely appropriate for the middle of town. I used to take him out of his stall to clean it and to walk him around. He was a bit spirited, and one spring day he suddenly jerked his head up and I lost the rope, at which point he wandered into the neighbor's yard and started munching on the lady's tulips. She was sort of a witch and had a fit about that, but she was not about to take on the horse. I don't think my parents cared much, except to avoid her wrath. (We used to tip over her trash cans at Halloween.)

The War Years

It was Sunday evening in Vermont on December 7, 1941, when we got first word of the Japanese attack on Pearl Harbor and the beginning of World War II (WWII) for the United States. I still remember the distinguished voice of President Roosevelt as we gathered around the one radio in the house to hear the news, when he made the famed "Day of Infamy" speech, declaring war on Japan.

It was feared there would be air raids, so all were required to have blackout curtains for the windows at night and citizens volunteered as Air Raid Wardens to patrol the streets to ensure no lights were showing. There was also gas rationing with big stickers on the windshield indicating how much gas you could buy. As a doctor who needed to drive across town to the hospital frequently, Dad rated an "A" sticker that allowed the purchase of four gallons per week. Food ration cards were also issued for sugar, coffee, meats, fats, milk, and cheese. It was a real treat to have sugar enough for a birthday cake!

Rubber was scarce and it was forbidden to buy tires for those four years, and some tires ended up being mostly patches! That was also a problem for bike riders. It was also a big blow to those of us building models of war planes since there were no rubber bands for the wind-up models.

There weren't enough doctors in town, so my father was exempt from the draft, and he continued his office practice. During the War we kept chicken coops in the carriage barn and had a "Victory Garden." There were a lot of chickens – Rhode Island Reds and White Leghorns. One of the roosters was nice and one was a devil who always chased me when I went into the cage. We enjoyed eating the devil at Thanksgiving. It was my job to collect the eggs and sell them to the neighbors. Sometimes a single egg ended up in my jacket pocket, and one night on the way home from choir practice at our church across town, a bully was taunting me as he raced away on his bicycle. I remembered the egg and lobbed it after him; it landed on the seat just as he sat down. That was a pleasant revenge.

My parents had driven to Florida during the coldest part of winter for several years, usually for a month or more. Because of gas rationing, we went on the train from Albany to Florida in 1943. The train was filled with men in uniform and quite crowded. We definitely didn't have Pullman accommodations! Another year, just after the end of the war, my mother drove from Vermont to Florida with me and my younger sister Elizabeth and Dad joined us later. Along the way, we got snowed in during an unusual blizzard in Rocky Mount, North Carolina. The hotels were full and food was scarce. We slept on the floor in the lobby of the hotel with a room full of other stranded travelers.

In Florida, we were enrolled in school. Some friends of my parents had a daughter who was a high school senior at the time. Even though I was in junior high school at the time, I developed a crush on her and (probably with parental nudging) asked her out to dinner. We were delivered to one of the fancier restaurants on the main street. I was dressed in coat and tie, in Florida weather, and probably sweating with fear as well. The young lady was very gracious, and she was the kind of person who probably didn't laugh at the whole thing later with friends.

Some other friends had a son about my age and I got an invitation to visit them in Wisconsin during the summer. My mother dropped me in Rice Lake, while she and her elderly uncle continued west to visit a relative in Idaho. The Wisconsin lakes were beautiful, and my hosts had a cabin on the lake. The fishing was spectacular, while the mosquitos were gigantic. With their coaching I caught my share of Northern Pike, and even a Muskellunge, which was a master predator in the freshwater lakes, and a spectacular fighter.

Holidays

Memorial Day

At the time there was an Old Soldiers' Home (now the Veterans' Home) near the edge of town. The old soldiers had a veranda with rocking chairs for a peaceful view of open fields and the surrounding hills. On Memorial Day every year there was a parade with the high school band marching through town, ending at the Soldiers' Home, where taps were played, and Lincoln's Gettysburg Address was recited. It was a nice thing for the old guys. I had the privilege of giving the address each year and probably could still do it without a cue card.

Fourth of July

In those days fireworks stores popped up on Main Street during the week before the 4th. They sold mostly strings of Chinese firecrackers to enthusiastic youngsters, as well as rockets and much larger "cherry bombs" which were quite dangerous. My Dad usually saw multiple cases of hand or eye injuries, some quite significant. Not yet graced with common sense, we had great ingenuity, placing the cherry bombs under a large tin can and blowing it 30 feet in the air. We learned not to do that with smaller Spam cans since they were blown into shrapnel. Another not-so-smart idea was to gather a bunch of the strike-anywhere match heads and put them between two carriage bolts screwed into one square nut, then drop them to the concrete, which ignited the match heads and boosted the whole thing high into the air. One could imagine that flying carriage bolts posed some hazard to those nearby.

GRANDPARENTS

My grandparents, Paul and Sophie, were immigrants from England. Paul was a weaver and during WWII he worked in a mill which produced tire fabric. His brother, ten years his junior, also was in the industry and had a hand in developing or introducing Jacquard looms to weave fancy damask cloth.

My father had a sister named Elizabeth, who died in infancy, and my sister and daughter carried the same name, but for some reason all of them were called "Suzie" to this day.

When my sister Suzie and I were young, my mother drove us to stay with the grandparents every summer for three or four weeks. Early on, they lived near the Point Street revolving bridge in Providence. They had a car, an old Packard, I think, but I don't think Paul ever took it out of the garage. He and I would often walk down to see the bridge rotate about its center axis to let ships pass up and down the river.

One time he was able to get permission to ride the bridge as it rotated, which was a great thrill for a little kid. Paul was always very nice, very English, and quiet. He usually called me "boy," especially if I was in trouble, but was very gentle. Sophie was much the opposite, always bustling, busy, loving us, and chiding us for bad behavior.

Sister Suzie, Dad, Mom, Paul, and Sophie.

A few years later they moved to Worcester for work in another woolen mill and lived in a three-story house on a corner at the top of a very steep hill on Orne Street. Paul always had corn flakes for breakfast and let them soak in milk until they were very soggy before he ate them. Then he walked down to the bus stop for the trip to work at the mill. Some afternoons my sister and I would walk down the hill to meet him, and maybe get an ice cream at the little store near the bus stop.

Sophie did all the laundry by hand in two slate sinks and hung it on a rotating clothesline three stories above ground. If any clothes were blown off the line, it was my job to descend four stories to the cellar to retrieve them. She took us with her when she walked down the hill to the A&P supermarket on Lincoln Street. Fortunately, the walk from there wasn't so steep since we had to walk home with all the groceries from the market.

We had a lot of fun those years in Worcester with my grandparents. They must have been in their 60's then but were always willing to walk up another hill to Green Hill Park for evening picnics. We always took stale bread to feed the large carp that lived there in the lake. They went crazy in the water fighting for the floating bread. There were no drink coolers then, so Sophie used to wrap the Coke bottles in wet newspaper to try to keep them cold.

During the warm days, my sister Suzie and I would walk up to a rec center with a lifeguard and rest rooms at the same lake. There was a rickety platform out in the lake with a diving board. We would take a sack lunch and stay for 3 or 4 hours. When the bells rang for Victory in Europe Day in 1945, I broke into tears, not for the victory, but for the fact that I was in the rest room and could never tell people where I was at the end of the war!

There were short-cuts to the swimming hole in the park, lined with poison ivy. Grandma would treat the painful itching with creosote in warm water – it smelled like telephone poles and turned the water into something that looked like a latté.

In their home, in the evenings, we would listen to the news and 15-minute radio programs like the Lone Ranger, Batman, and war news. One favorite was about a couple of fliers called Hop Hadrian and Tank Tinker during the War.

Sometimes Paul and Sophie would listen to comedy shows after dinner, but usually we played cards or board games with them until bedtime.

On rare occasions, Sophie would take us into the center of Worcester on the bus for shopping and a movie. When the movie Fantasia came out, I guess I must have been old enough to take the bus by myself because I remember being in trouble for staying to see the movie a second time. By the time the second show was over, it was well into the night, and everyone was very worried.

Paul's twin sister Pauline lived alone in Rhode Island and would visit while we were there. She was an extremely timid spinster lady and my sister and I would scare her by hiding in the heavy velveteen drapes between the living room and the dining room, then jump out shouting "Boo!" No matter how often we did it, she would scream and go tell Sophie she had to do something about "those children."

Paul's youngest brother, Uncle Victor, lived in Rhode Island and had a big yacht with two inboard engines. I remember more about polishing and painting than about fishing although sometimes he took us on trips into Narragansett Bay on the boat. Uncle Victor got sunburned very easily and always wore long shirts and a big hat, no matter the weather. He was very funny and told corny jokes all the time.

The Iceman

Sophie and Paul didn't have a refrigerator, a washer or dryer, and either no hot water or not much, because Sophie would boil a kettle of water and carry it into the bathroom just off the kitchen for our baths. One time I guess I was running around with no clothes on and ran into her as she was carrying the kettle and got scalded. It must not have been too bad since there were no scars.

Instead of a refrigerator, most people had ice boxes, with a big block of ice in the top compartment, and circular shelves below that which would rotate so you could find the stuff in back. Nothing was very cold, but it allowed us to keep vegetables and milk for a few days. Ice cream was a problem, because it got soft on the walk home from the store anyway, and the ice didn't keep it frozen, so usually we had a popsicle at the little corner store by the bus stop where Grandpa got off. As the block of ice melted, one had to get rid of the water. I don't remember exactly how it worked, but I think there was a big pan underneath the ice box which had to be emptied every day.

Ice was delivered daily if needed. A diamond shaped sign marked 25#, 50#, 75#, or 100# was placed in the bedroom window facing the street. Seeing this, a man with a big ice pick and a rubber shield on his back would lug the large cake of ice up three flights for us.

Post War

After 1945, things gradually returned to normal for adults and kids. We used to play soldier, or whatever games were suggested, in the woods behind the next-door neighbor's house in Bennington. The slope was quite steep, and there was a slender tree, which we treated like Tarzan's vine, and we would swing on it as it bent to the ground below.

Most of the town could be explored on bicycles; there was an ice cream shop on Main Street, near Dad's office, and a drug store with a dairy fountain and a marble counter near the corner of Valentine and Main Streets, across from a lovely old brick building, the Baptist church.

A big family with lots of kids lived in a ramshackle house in an alley off Valentine Street. There was a concrete parking space facing the alley across the street. It was ideal for games of hide and seek or a variation called "kick the can" during the long summer evenings until well after dark. One evening when I ran out of the alley into the street, I was struck by a car, and ended up lying on the hood, eye to eye with the driver. I wasn't hurt and ran off to hide. When I returned 10 minutes later, the poor man was still sitting in the same place, apparently in shock. "Shoulda been dead."

After school, the Valentine mob and the rest of the neighborhood boys gathered most afternoons, playing soldier, football, or bike riding. My mother worried that the boys might be a bad influence, but they were good friends and we played high school football together for four years.

Even when we were in primary school, it was quite safe for my sister and me to walk across town to class. The school was next to a small river called The Roaring Branch which only roared with the spring floods. It was fenced but all the kids got to the river to play anyway. It was probably contaminated by the woolen mill upstream, but that wasn't much of an issue in those days.

When I was in third grade a bully got in a fight with me and gave me a bloody nose. My sister, two years younger, was very protective of me and as a small child with a glint in her eye would take on anyone who threatened me. I don't remember if she was there for that incident, but I appreciated her concern. There was only one more fist fight, in high school with another unpleasant bully at the bike rack; I prevailed in that one.

Primary school was divided – the Irish and French Catholic kids went to different primary and middle schools. Those of us in public school moved to the Bennington High School building in 7th grade, and the Catholic kids joined us for high school.

In those days the girls in junior high often called the boys repeatedly in the evenings. I pictured my caller as a little mousy kid with stringy hair, and sort of played cool and disregarded her. You could imagine my mortification when the most gorgeous red head I have ever seen came up to me in high school, and by way of introduction said, "Hi, I'm Mary Jane. Do you remember that silly crush I had on you in junior high?" So much for "cool." She also wore green undies on St. Patrick's Day and gave the class a glimpse of those.

Later my dad told me he heard she had passed away with melanoma. Thirty years later at our high school reunion, my wife and I were browsing the gift shop in the hotel where we were staying, and suddenly Mary Jane appeared from behind the counter, not a ghost, and still a beautiful woman.

During the class banquet, a woman who had been the editor of the school newspaper mentioned to my wife that she didn't think I'd ever amount to much.

When I was in junior high school, we moved outside of town to Windylea, a bucolic place on 40 acres, including a house without indoor plumbing, a hand pump for drinking water, a carriage house, and a real barn across the street with stalls for 30 cows at one time. Later, there was a box stall for my horse. At the upper level was a hayloft, just right for jumping from the rafters into the hay. Much later, my pals and their girlfriends seemed to be drawn to jumping in the hay as well.

As I gained more experience caring for the horse and riding, I was able to wander the 40 acres which came with the farm. My dad bought my sister another horse and when they were on the hill across the brook, I could whistle, and they would come at a canter for carrots they knew were hidden in my pockets.

There was a basketball hoop in the barn. During the school year I used to practice during the freezing nights after school, but never got good enough to make the team. Football was more promising, and the coach put me in as a lineman. The football coach was a Marine drill sergeant type, and the older and more portly head coach was rumored to have an interest in the head cheerleader. Apparently, scandal wasn't invented recently!

The home had been a working farm originally, until the "old man" was gored by his pet bull, leaving his wife to fend for herself. At that time the dwelling was two structures with a gap between them, bedrooms in front, and kitchen and pantry in back. The widow divided the front rooms into much smaller bedrooms for boarders and survived that way.

The house at Windylea.

After we bought it, Dad directed a drastic makeover. He removed the cistern tank for water collection in the cellar and the hand pump lifting water from the spring down in the brook. The pot belly stoves were replaced with central heating. The two segments of the house were connected, and the gap between buildings became a spacious dining room with a memorable view both north and south. A breakfast room and a half bath were added in the kitchen area. Dad decided on the size of the bathroom by dragging in a toilet, sitting on it with elbows spread to measure the width of the room. There were closets for winter clothes at the back door, and a China closet in the passageway to the new dining room. My mother used to keep her wedding and engagement rings in a glass in that closet. One day during the remodel, her rings disappeared, and one of the workmen was the prime suspect. A year later, the rings just as mysteriously reappeared when some other work was being done. We later surmised they had been "borrowed" then "returned." Such was the morality of folks in a small town.

It was a little over a mile from home to the high school on Main Street, and I rode my bike in summer and winter. The Buick dealer's home was on Morgan Street, the only route to school. He had two Dobermans that always chased me. I learned to get up speed, then coast past his house with my feet on the handlebars until the dogs tired of the chase. Often, I rode my bike even when the snow was 8 to 9" thick on the road.

No matter the weather, Dad rarely took us to school in his Chevrolet convertible, but I do remember one morning he drove me to school, with the top down, the wind blowing, and the temperature near zero.

Freddy

It was a new experience to learn about life in the country but fortunately Dad had a large family of patients, farmers who lived just across the valley. Their son Freddy helped us to cut and gather hay, among a myriad of other kindnesses. One day I was riding my horse up the hill where Freddy was cutting the hay for us in an old orchard with a horse drawn sickle mower. He stopped work for a minute for a drink of water and a few words, while I sat on my horse. Suddenly a bee from the nearby apple tree stung my horse, which reared up like they did in the cowboy movies, and one of his front hooves came down on my friend's skull, knocking him unconscious. That blow could have killed him, but this guy was a tough Vermont farm kid.

As he gradually revived, I implored him to come down the hill to let my father examine him, but he climbed back on the rig and went back to work, saying "My Dad will whup me if I don't finish this field today." Fortunately, he did not suffer any long-term consequences, but the scene is still remembered.

Tragedy

There was a fatal accident which occurred when two older ladies were out for a ride in the country nearby. The road past our house came down a steep grade, made a 90-degree turn and crossed the brook which followed the path of a long-forgotten trolley line between Pownal and Bennington.

Coming down the hill, they lost control and tipped over. This was long before the days of seat belts, and the driver was thrown, and crushed between the door and the road. There was no 911 at that time, and my father, the doctor, was miles away at the office. She was a hefty woman, and as best as I could tell as a middle school kid, she was quite dead. A call was made to the police, and rescuers came, and took the distraught survivor away. We didn't see any of the subsequent events, being shooed away into the house by my mother.

Sugaring Off

Up the hill from our home, there was a good stand of maple trees. I tapped the trees in the spring and carried the buckets of sap down the hill and we then boiled the sap on the kitchen stove until it thickened into delicious maple syrup. The farm neighbors were my father's patients, and they always had a "sugaring off" party, as it was called, at the end of the syrup season and invited friends and neighbors to join them.

The syrup was boiled until it turned into a sort of taffy when spooned onto a dish of snow, to be eaten with sticky fingers. It was very sweet, and the mother of this large family served homemade doughnuts, pickles to balance the sweetness, and strong coffee, made in one of those huge, galvanized coffee pots on a wood stove.

When everyone had enough sweet stuff, the kids were allowed to stir the thickened syrup in a cereal bowl until it turned into maple cream, which is often sold in maple leaf shapes at the souvenir shops. Those honest people, the odor of the boiling syrup, and the faint smell of muddy barn boots lingers.

Sweet!

Blanchards

When we moved into Windylea, there were concerns about our water supply from the spring in the brook because the neighbors upstream by the bridge had an outhouse on the edge of the brook, as well as pigs and cows. Dad got a 5-foot diameter clay cylinder, and had it installed over the bubbling spring at our edge of the brook; the water always tested "safe."

The couple, John Blanchard and his wife Minnie, lived there – no children that I recall. John taught me a lot about hard work and life. Dad hired him to build a fence for our two horses around the large pasture which went from the bridge up the hill to a maple grove, and back down the east side across the brook to the barn, perhaps six or seven acres in all.

John was a lean, tough old farmer, and standing on his wagon with a huge sledgehammer we drove those fence posts into the rocky Vermont soil for a full day. I was playing football at the time, and in good shape, but I was exhausted long before we quit. John seemed fresh as a daisy.

During high school years, we would sit on the front steps of their house in the evenings, and chat; actually, I would ask questions, since John was a laconic Vermonter who rarely started a conversation. He said that he had never traveled more than 70 miles from home, and on only one or two occasions, although they had a car.

Blanchard home.

When asked about the movies in town, he said they had gone once around 1920, but didn't think enough of it to go again. He tried to teach me how to milk their two cows, but I wasn't very good at it, and it was really tiring for the fingers and wrists. The cows could produce a good-sized stainless pail half full of milk, which was carried into the house and run through a De Laval cream separator they had in an alcove off the dining room. Mrs. Blanchard was a good cook, and her whipped cream cakes were wonderful. The cream from the separator was so rich that it hardly needed to be whipped. Mom was horrified, since the milk was "raw milk" and in the days before WWII, raw milk sometimes carried tuberculosis.

They also had some fruit trees, grew vegetables in a garden across the brook, and got meat from the pigs, so were pretty much self-sustaining. I really respected their lifestyle and life philosophy.

Long after I left Bennington, they both passed on, and my mother purchased the house for Paul and Sophie and modernized it a bit. There were pleasant days there with them as well. One year our family celebrated Thanksgiving at their house. Sophie had cooked a big turkey and was bringing the turkey in on a platter to the dining room; she slipped on some grease, fell on her backside, and the turkey went skidding into the corner. Fortunately, she wasn't injured, and when we recovered her and the turkey, we had a good laugh and a good turkey dinner.

High School

The high school years were complicated. Besides a new level of academic expectations, there were new social issues, dating, dances, and sports. Everyone took lunch boxes, complete with a Thermos of milk.

My best friend, Jack Evans and I would sit on the cellar windowsill of the janitor's office and ponder the world. Jack became a Catholic scholar and a professor at Arizona State, while I pursued a Navy career. We were both straight A students in all our required courses. Vying for valedictorian senior year, Jack protected a straight A record by taking one less course than I. My downfall was a Civics elective course with a teacher who never gave an A, so I ended up with one B, and the same number of A's as Jack, who was valedictorian, and I settled for salutatorian.

Yearbook photo.

Bennington High School was blessed with excellent teachers in English, Math, French, Chemistry, Civics, and "Home Economics," which included typing and sewing for those headed for secretarial or home duties. In those pre-computer days, typing was a valuable skill, not recognized by most male students; it was a recommended class for college-bound kids, and it turned out to be one of the most useful for me.

Although I wasn't a football star, I was good enough to travel with the team, and reconnected with Betty, a girl I had met earlier at a church camp at the bishop's estate on Lake Champlain. The team traveled to Barre, Vermont, for a game, and they offered to put me up at Betty's home. Her mother had firm ideas about high school boys and kept a stern eye on me whenever I had a chance to visit. The mistrust couldn't have been too deep though. I still have a beautiful red ski sweater she knitted for me, as well as a matching ski cap.

That long-distance friendship persisted through college, into our later years when she had moved to Reno after a couple of not-so-successful choices of husbands. Betty and my wife Sadako became good friends, and we visited when we could, until she passed away.

When we had access to an automobile, we would drive around with friends on school days during lunch hour. During senior year, my parents were away during the spring, leaving me their car for transportation to school for me and my younger sister. One might anticipate that this would lead to "outings" of which they wouldn't have approved.

One fine spring day, six of us seniors piled into Dad's Chevy convertible and drove up into the mountains on a two-lane winding road. Rather than sightseeing, the goal was to see how fast the car would go coming down the mountain, with the top down, and the wind blowing through the girls' hair in the back seat.

Speeding down the two-lane mountain road, we hit 93 mph, impressive for cars of that era! As we slowed for a light on Main Street, however, a tire blew! There was no problem quickly changing the tire, but in the process, I noticed that there were multiple layers of tire cord showing on all four tires, any one of which could have dumped us into the river or onto boulders that day. I was quite perturbed that my father would let things slide to that degree and was humbled by my recklessness.

My Dad shared interesting stories about unusual patients. One couple reminded us of an old English poem which went:

> Jack Sprat could eat no fat.
> His wife could eat no lean.
> And so between them both, you see,
> They licked the platter clean.

The lady (we'll call her "Fanny") was quite corpulent, and during pregnancy measuring her weight gain was a problem. The office scales of the day only went to 350 pounds, and since she was a bit over 400, my dad sent her down to the coal company to be weighed on their truck scales,

Curiously, she had a penchant for young boys. She also had a tiny Chevy two door coupe. As innocent boys too young to drink in Vermont, four of us classmates would sneak away to the State Line Bar just across the border in New York, have one beer, talk, get giddy, and get home sober.

Certainly, we all were virgins at the time. One night while we were nursing our illegal beers, Fanny's Chevy showed up, she strode in and whispered into the ear of one of the boys. They retired to her car, which bounced around for a bit, then our friend returned with a silly grin on his face. We all breathlessly questioned him, "Didya, Didya?" To which he responded, "I think so!" He later became a Catholic priest. We did speculate about cause and effect.

Often a group of friends would gather on South Street at one of our classmate's homes to chat and share news. I remember one guy who used to lie on the floor and read from the Montgomery Ward catalog, usually odd items, or lingerie ads.

During senior year, I worked at an estate near the Bennington Battle Monument in the morning, and at Fairdale Farms dairy bar and restaurant in the afternoon and evening. My grandparents lived in a little stone house, the gatehouse for a mansion near the Farms. For football training, I would run from the estate to my grandparent's house for lunch and a shower, then walk to Fairdale Farms, which was a large dairy farm serving the entire community, first from horse-drawn wagons then later from delivery trucks. The milk was not homogenized, so the cream rose to the top. Someone had come up with an ingenious milk bottle design with a constriction about 4 inches from the top, and special spoons, so the cream could be poured off.

The Farm was situated on the main road to New York state and brought big business on holiday weekends. There were also weekend summer nights spent square-dancing behind the restaurant on a large rink originally designed for skating. I enjoyed working there and the perks of free ice cream were nice.

My job was behind the ice cream counter, where two of us served customers in the yard through a pass-through window, prepared sundaes, and served meals to customers sitting at the counter. We also made shakes, sodas, and sundaes for the waitresses handling the adjacent dining room.

One frantically busy summer afternoon, my "colleague," a theatrical sort of guy, was taking a luxurious lunch break at a table across from the counter while I tried to keep up. The vanilla ice cream drum was empty, and I yelled for help. His response was "I should care!" which thoroughly infuriated me. I grabbed a frozen scoop of ice cream from the bottom of the cooler and flung it at him across the aisle. A man and his wife chose precisely that moment to walk between us, and the lady took the frozen missile in her ear. She was unhurt, but the cold ice cream in one ear gave her severe vertigo, and she sank to the floor. Her husband lunged, and chaos reigned for a bit. After order was restored, the manager, an imposing large lady, took us into her office for an explanation. To my surprise, we were chastised but not fired.

My dad paid for some golf lessons for me at the Mt. Anthony Country Club, but after days of doing nothing but chipping balls on the fifth fairway it got old. It did lead to a job as a caddy at the club, with the added benefit of use of the swimming pool early in the day. Trying to do flips off the diving board and landing flat on your back was painful, so a (bad) idea came to mind -- doing the flip off the edge of the concrete walk. Starting too far away from the edge I hit my head on the deck and awoke somewhat later at the bottom of the pool. Chalk up another one for the "Shoulda been dead" list.

During senior year a new girl named Dolly showed up; she was living with the family of a guy who had been called away for Army National Guard duty during the Korean war. They were either seriously dating or engaged. Since I was technically "attached" to the girl in Barre, a hundred miles away, and she to the Army guy we hung around together during school activities like drama club, dances, and group parties. Things got a little dicey when we went to a house party of a classmate out in the country and had to wake a farmer to pull our car out of a field. He was helpful and kind, but said, "Ain't you Doc Browning's kid?"

The high school yearbook had an "ambition" and "prognostication" next to our pictures. Mine said my ambition was "Navy pilot" but the prognostication was "Race Car Driver." Her ambition was "Army wife" and prognostication "Navy Widow." Too much mischief by the editors!

Sal

During high school, I got a job working in a Sunoco service station directly across from the courthouse. We provided a full range of automotive services, as well as condoms out of a closet for kids worried their parents might find out if they bought them at a drug store. The owner, Sal, was a spunky Italian guy who spun tales about WWII, was a patient boss, and a good teacher and counselor, who taught me about life, as well as automobiles.

One guy just out of high school worked nights at the station and bought a 1939 Cadillac V-12 limousine for $175. The widow lady who owned it originally had kept it up on blocks during the war, so it was in beautiful condition. He got a mechanic out of retirement to tune it up, thus raising the gas mileage from 4 mpg to a whopping 8 mpg! It did need four new mufflers. The regional supplier must have thought they were for some potentate, and mailed them by air, which cost more than the car.

He was a very tall young man and had a girlfriend who was quite diminutive. The car had a glass partition between the front and back seats; he bought a chauffeur's outfit and drove around town with his date perched in the back seat behind the partition until they ran out of gas (and money).

There was also a nice 1932 Pierce Arrow automobile parked in front of the station and it was for sale for $100. However, it needed engine work and when it was started a cloud of smoke enveloped the street as well as the courthouse opposite. We got a "cease and desist" order from the judge, who will be mentioned later in another interaction.

Sal and his wife and children always went to mass on Sunday in his beautiful 1941 Cadillac. He usually stopped by after church to check on things, since I was running the station alone on weekends. During the summer, traffic was heavy, with no "self-service," and no automatic shut-off pumps. There were no credit cards so you carried a pad of duplicate charge slips, on which the amount and cost was noted and signed by the driver. Managing four pumps kept me jumping, and one Sunday I left the pad of charge slips on the roof of a car as it drove off. In a panic, I left the shop and gave chase, without success. When I returned Sal and his wife in Sunday finery were waiting in the Caddy, not pleased at the abandoned service station. Since the pad of receipts was the only record of the day's sales, it was critical to have them. He drove off in search as well and found them scattered in a field a few miles away. I should have been fired, but wasn't, and only suffered a few harsh words.

When it wasn't busy, Sal would let me use the equipment for work on my mother's car. Anticipating a trip to the beach in New Hampshire, I got permission from my parents to get four new tires for the convertible. Sal was using the hydraulic lift, so I unwisely decided to use two floor jacks, one under the front frame and the other under the differential box in the rear to lift the car off the ground. Things went well until I removed the fourth wheel, at which point the car tipped to one side onto the wheel hubs, ending up only inches from the plate glass window of the show room. Responding to my panic, Sal walked over, looked, and said only, "You silly son of a bitch!"

Sal set a good example for the teens who hung around the station. Later he took over the heating oil service for the town, and eventually became a state senator, with a nice home on the prestigious Bennington Monument Circle.

During senior year I bought a 2-door 1932 Ford Model B sedan for $70. It was a transitional model between the classic 4-cylinder Model A and the more powerful V-8s developed six months later. There weren't many around, and parts were a problem. The front seats tilted forward for access to the back seats. The floor underneath the seats had partially rusted out, and the plywood replacement wasn't quite adequate, so the passenger's seat was very low.

One day, Miss Hutton, the French teacher was walking home across town, and I offered her a ride. She was a very proper lady, but accepted with a smile, and got into the passenger seat with her pile of books in her lap. I still remember the formal expression on her face sitting primly and chatting politely, with the top of her head barely up to window level.

Vintage Ford Model B.

The car was rickety in other ways; one afternoon my group of friends piled in for a spin, and as we went over a railroad crossing, the battery bounced out of the battery case, only hanging on by its positive and negative cables. The engine seemed unfazed.

It was always good for a ride during lunch hour. At noon one day a couple of us went for a spin around Old Bennington, which had one ancient policeman who was retained mostly to discourage "riffraff" from entering the stately neighborhood. As we sedately circled the monument, we suddenly had the old cop in hot pursuit, not happy to see a couple of high school kids in an old clunker, so he cited us for speeding. Even though it was difficult to exceed 15 mph on that circle without rolling over, we had to go to court. We researched the length of the straight section, the G-forces involved in making the turns (the "circle" was really a square with rounded corners), and measured the maximum acceleration of the vehicle, and went into court accompanied by my father, armed with all sorts of facts and figures. The highly respected judge knew everyone in town and was friends with most. Fortunately, he didn't treat us as "smart alecks," and listened with a straight face to all our assertions and calculations. I don't remember the outcome, but it was most likely an admonition, or possibly some community service. The old cop didn't look happy with the outcome.

Another day during lunch break, for some reason we decided to remove the fan from the Ford at Sal's garage. In our haste to get back to school, the key holding the fan in place was missing, and the fan came loose and "ate" the radiator. Repairs weren't feasible and the search for a replacement was unsuccessful; the radiator continued to sit in the back seat. The car could go short distances before overheating, so I could still drive to school. When it did overheat, it would run on or "diesel" after shutting off the ignition and backfire a few times before settling down. Not only did this announce my arrival when I was late to school, but the backfiring tended to disrupt classes. After I got permission to drive into the school yard and park with the car in gear against a tree, that did prevent the engine from running on. Only when the coil melted did it truly stop running. However, even in that condition I sold it for my original purchase price of $70!

Winter Misadventure

During Christmas break of our freshman college year, a group of five or six of us met over coffee and decided to go camping overnight up in the nearby mountains. Too bad common sense wasn't a requirement to be a college student. Had we done a weather check, we might have noticed that the temperature would be well below zero in town, and 8 to 10 degrees colder on the mountain.

I took a sleeping bag and hiking boots, but most had tennis shoes and blankets. An older friend, familiar with the trails, did guide us to a logging hut, but was wise enough not to stay. By nightfall it was bitter cold and the chimney of the stove, which had been used for target practice in the past, spewed more smoke than heat. Our menu was Spam and potatoes on metal plates, and we had only one frying pan. While the meat charred on one side, it was still frozen on the other. Trying to rinse the plates in a mountain brook, they immediately picked up a coat of ice.

Darkness came early, we tried to sleep and conserve warmth. My boots were so stiff that I had to put them in the sleeping bag to warm them enough to get them on in the morning. Another guy nearly got a concussion when the guy in the bunk above dropped a frozen potato on him. We hiked out shortly after first light and had breakfast at a restaurant back in Bennington. My mother had kept vigil at home during the night, spied the wisp of smoke from the cabin, and said the temperature in town was -20 degrees, and probably 5 to 10 degrees colder up on the mountain.

My parents took me to Dartmouth during high school for an introduction to the college. Attendance was preordained, however, since my dad had applied for me the year I was born and there was a NROTC (Naval Reserve Officers' Training Corps) unit offering tuition assistance as well. I was quite happy with that prospect. Security and pomp and circumstance were certainly more low-key in those days. President Eisenhower was the graduation speaker one year, and it was possible to get some close-up pictures of the great man on the dais in front of Webster Library.

Eisenhower at Webster Library.

My mother drove me to school in September and helped me to find used furniture for a two-room suite in Ripley Hall, one of the dormitories on campus. My roommate, Charlie Greenebaum, was a much more sophisticated fellow from New York City. His dad also applied for him at birth and was in the same class as my dad.

We were all required to eat at the college dining hall during freshman year. Dad paid for that and gave me a $2 food stipend after that. Most of us chose to spend the $2 on groceries for clandestine cooking in our rooms since restaurant choices were limited.

There was also a Navy stipend of $50 a month, most of which was saved for dates, rather than food!

Dartmouth College Winter
Carnival Snow Statue.

Baker Library, modeled after
Independence Hall in Philadelphia.

Midshipman Cruises

First Summer – 1952

The 1952 summer active-duty cruise for NROTC students from Dartmouth was aboard the USS Saipan, an aircraft carrier commissioned at the end of WWII. The midshipmen assigned were from several colleges, and we were berthed in one cavernous compartment housing 240 students. We all carried aboard duffel bags with prescribed uniforms, enlisted type whites with the old "dixie cup" hats. This round white cap worn by sailors had a blue rim around the cap that designated the wearer as an officer in training. The enlisted men told the girls in port that the blue stripe indicated the wearer had a venereal disease! That seemed like taking unfair advantage of the dating situation! Dungarees were for workdays at sea, and officer type dress blues for shore excursions. Even underwear was prescribed, boxer shorts with bows at the sides because elastic wouldn't survive the ship's laundry.

The folding canvas bunks were stacked five high, and the clearance was not quite enough to roll over without waking the man above. When reveille was sounded, 240 middies leapt out of their "racks" simultaneously. Getting dressed when the ship was pitching was a bit dicey. Sometimes the deck would be wet in the berthing area, so it was a trick to get into white pants without getting the cuffs dirty.

There was a large common shower room, with probably 20 to 30 shower heads, sometimes delivering sea water if fresh water was scarce. The bathroom facilities were also somewhat primitive, with 8 or 10 toilet seats bolted onto a trough with continuous running sea water, and not much in the way of privacy.

Meals were served on compartmented steel trays, on long folding tables for 10 to 12 people. One time in rough weather, the legs on one end collapsed, and 10 trays of food went sliding down into the lap of the midshipman seated at the end of the table!

The senior enlisted enjoyed the opportunity to "initiate" the innocents, and I remember we were assigned by a Chief Petty Officer to polish the urinals with Brasso, more commonly used to polish brass belt buckles. In spite of these humiliations, the cruise was educational, eventful, and exciting. During the first few days, the weather in the North Atlantic was stormy, and many of the students were seasick. I remember that because those of us who weren't sick were allowed to have 3 or 4 desserts, a rare treat. Overall, the food was pretty good.

We rotated assignments during the trip, in gunnery, engineering, and navigation. The gunnery exercises, firing 40-mm antiaircraft guns was exciting, and keeping them loaded was heavy work. We each got some time in the gunner's seat during the period, controlling the guns and firing at targets.

First visit to Torquay, England.

The navigation rotation gave us an opportunity to stand watch on the bridge and learn the skill of using a sextant to calculate the location of the ship, and to watch flight operations if they were going on.

The aircraft on board were older than expected; F6F Hellcat fighters, the Grumman TBM Avenger, and a WWII torpedo bomber with three crew members. In one case we witnessed, the crew included a pilot, a navigator, and a flight surgeon in the bottom turret position, (along to get his flight time.) The pilot couldn't make a successful landing and had to ditch in the water alongside the carrier. The problem was that the guy in the bottom turret position had to get out through the bottom hatch, which was going to be underwater as they landed. There was a lot of speculation and joking among the sailors on deck: apparently the flight surgeon hadn't been popular for bringing everyone's immunizations up to date. In this case everything worked out okay, and all three escaped and were picked up uninjured.

We made port in Torquay, England, which was a very nice port. The countryside was lovely, and the Lord Mayor hosted a dance with many local young ladies in attendance; we all quickly learned to waltz again. Things were quite tightly chaperoned, but the young lady I had as a dance partner suggested three of us midshipmen might rent a car the next day and explore the countryside with three of them. The ladies made arrangements for the refreshments and took us to the British equivalent of the DMV where we got visitors' licenses with remarkably little fuss. The stormy Atlantic was left behind, and we had a very pleasant day in the country with three very charming companions. As a matter of fact, my new friend met me two years later when we returned to England on the senior midshipman cruise.

From Torquay we sailed to Dublin, Ireland, for the second port stop, with similar hospitality. We were told that the Saipan was the first aircraft carrier ever to sail into the River Liffey in the heart of Dublin. Another charming memory was a stop in a pub in uniform. When I ordered a Guinness Stout, a dark beer brewed in Dublin, an elderly lady sitting near me at the bar immediately turned to me and said, "No, no, laddie, you've got to drink it 'arf and 'arf (half and half with a lighter beer), apparently convinced I was too young for the "real" stuff.

On the return trip from the British Isles, we sailed to the U.S. Naval Base at Guantanamo Bay. At that time relations with Cuba were not good. The Navy, in particular, was unwelcome after some tipsy sailor relieved himself on a statue in town. This meant that leaving the base was not an option.

The final rotation for us was in the engine rooms and the fire rooms, which made the base seem like a winter vacation. The temperatures in the fire rooms were often 105 to 110 degrees. Even so, the "Snipes" as the men in the boiler rooms and engine rooms were known, constantly drank coffee made by venting high pressure 600-degree steam through a copper coil immersed in a large metal coffee pot.

There wasn't much of note about the cruise from there back to Norfolk, and it was good to get back to Vermont before the fall semester started.

Second Summer – 1953

The second year was split between amphibious warfare training in Norfolk, Virginia, and exposure to aviation in Corpus Christi, Texas. During the Virginia segment, I was introduced to a very attractive nursing student in Norfolk who was an adventurous type. She taught me the art of stealing crabs in the bay from her boat, before revealing that the owners often shot the thieves if they caught them. Hmmm.

I was hoping to get into aviation and looking forward to the tour in Corpus Christi. For some reason, though, I had a strong premonition of impending death, which I never had before, nor since. I shared this with my lady friend, but not my parents. Before we left Norfolk, I did call them to say goodbye though, which they thought was a bit odd.

The flight from Norfolk to Corpus Christi was in an old R4Q (Air Force C-119) two engine transport holding 50 or 60 passengers. Our group of around 50 midshipmen from Dartmouth and Princeton lined up on the tarmac, gazing at the airplane with the cowling off one engine. Not a big confidence builder. The crew finished repairs and loaded us aboard, pointing out that the old flying boxcar wasn't luxury travel. We deplaned in Corpus and started the exciting aviation half of the summer. However, tragedy did strike later. The very same aircraft crashed on take-off after a refueling stop, while carrying a group of midshipmen from Rice, killing all but three on board.

After our exciting 4 to 6 weeks in the aviation community, four of us decided to drive home after the cruise. A Marine major sold us an older Oldsmobile and said it was a great car. We handed over most of our remaining cash and departed. As I recall, three of our group were from the Chicago area, another from Ohio, while I was returning to Vermont. The trip started well; we slept in farmer's fields along the way, since our meager finances mandated a spartan trip and cheap food.

Sometime around the second or third day, the automatic transmission started slipping and we found we were out of oil. We figured that some fluid and sealing additive should readily solve the problem, but it continued to worsen and by the time with got into Illinois, we were pouring cheap motor oil through the filler, which was conveniently located on the floor near the right front seat.

The car finally gave up the ghost on a back road in farming country and, after briefly debating what would happen if we abandoned it, we picked up our duffle bags, said goodbye, and put our thumbs out. I was fortunate, catching a ride nearly all the way home to Vermont from somewhere in Indiana or Ohio.

Third Summer – 1954

The itinerary was much the same as the previous cruise with stops in Portsmouth, England; Dublin, Ireland; and Guantanamo, but the ship was far different. A small contingent of us were assigned to the USS Loeser, an old destroyer escort out of Norfolk. Of course, the names varied between Loeser, Looser, and Loser. The crew was much smaller, at 213, compared with over 900 on the Saipan.

Midshipman life was a bit better as we were more seasoned with the previous cruise experience. Due to the difference in size, we bounced around a lot more than we had on the aircraft carrier. The duty rotations were about the same, with exposure to navigation, engineering, and gunnery, although we were given more responsibility due to the smaller crew and previous experience.

The diesel-electric propulsion was quite different, since steam was used to turn an electric motor driving the two propellers, compared with the Saipan which had four screws and steam turbines. The crew used to joke that if we sprung a leak, we would all be electrocuted. The ship was in the later part of her career and was a bit "tired." The crew swore that a sailor was chipping paint below the waterline one day, struck his head on the metal above, cursed, swung a mighty blow, and went right through the rusted hull. None of these stories could be corroborated, of course.

Portsmouth was a good city to visit, and we were treated well by the folks there. We all went on a bus tour in Ireland, and did not see as much of Dublin, but the country certainly earned its reputation as the Emerald Isle.

The visit to Guantanamo was vastly more colorful than the first trip. Four destroyers were tied up together abreast, so that it might be necessary to cross the decks of three destroyers before reaching your own.

There were sentries to control access, but they were no match for the carousers returning after a night at the Club. The sentry on the first deck apparently challenged a returning sailor, and was tossed overboard, carbine and all, and mostly was encouraged to keep the weapon above water. There also seemed to be some indignation about other sailors invading the sanctity of our deck, and several more were tossed in the drink.

I was in the engineering division at that time, and apparently the crew thought I was okay. When we were ready to go ashore, I found a Machinist Mate First class jumper on my bunk, rather than the humble midshipman style. This allowed me to party with the "real guys" at the enlisted club. I was highly grateful for the honor and remember most of the evening as being quite enjoyable. (The remainder I don't remember.)

Gigi

There was a summer break from Dartmouth after the cruise and I got a job doing yard work for a wealthy woman who lived on the prestigious "Monument Circle" around the Bennington Battle Monument. She was a good friend of my mother's, and they arranged a date with a young woman from Bennington College. She was a beautiful fragile lady who my friends called "The China Doll." She was a gifted pianist, and quite pleasant company. We had a few dinner dates, but nothing serious developed.

Things changed dramatically when she arranged a double date for a fraternity friend from Dartmouth. His date, Gigi, decided she had different plans for the day. I was driving my Dad's Buick convertible through the center of Bennington with my pianist friend in the front seat, and fraternity brother and Gigi in the back seat. As we approached the center of town, frat brother's date suddenly stood up in the back seat, leaned over the driver's seat, and planted a big kiss on my forehead. We didn't crash or run a red light, but the dating arrangements certainly changed quickly.

Thus began two memorable years, and a very brief engagement. When I introduced my new date from Bennington to a fraternity brother during the Green Key spring weekend, he was a bit taken aback when she dipped her fingers into his martini, stole the olive, popped it in her mouth, then wiped her fingers on his necktie.

On another occasion, a group of us had a picnic on the banks of the Queeche Gorge, a roaring flume during the spring snow melt which emptied into the Connecticut River. My date, in her bikini, was flirting again, and my response to that was that it seemed a good idea to go body surfing in the roaring river. The current carried me over huge boulders the size of Volkswagens and dragged me down far enough that it became momentarily dark. My date and friends trotted along the shore and when I finally reached dry ground, an old farmer was looking appreciatively at my date, and offered a towel at his home nearby. After joining us for a few beers he was ready to pass out, Gigi helped lug him into his house, ignored his wife, and pulled another beer out of their refrigerator. All in all, it was an unusual day.

One year my sister came to Winter Carnival. My lady friend and I had just returned to my dorm room on the ground floor of the dorm when my sister climbed through the window, plunked herself in a chair, and asked for a drink. That pretty much eliminated any chance of immediate romance.

Medical School became a future goal, and the Navy would not allow scholarship holders to take any pre-med courses, since it might lead to early departure for medical school as soon as the Navy obligation was finished. Thus, it was necessary for those of us considering medicine to find alternative sources for the med school admission requirements.

One mandatory requirement was a semester course in comparative anatomy. Someone put me in touch with an affable science professor at Bennington College who was willing to offer an individual study program during the summer to fulfill that requirement in exchange for a new telescopic sight for his deer rifle. It sounded good to me, and the course turned out to be interesting and educational. The summer job working with the grounds crew at the college was also welcome.

Driving a gang mower over the luxurious lawns, I had pretty much full-time permission to be on campus. Bennington College was 99 percent female students at that time, so the scenery while working was usually most pleasant, although occasionally one might come around a corner to find a couple frolicking in the summer sun and need to take emergency avoidance measures.

These conditions were ideal for romance to flourish. The dorms were open to visitors, so my unconventional friend and I were able to share thoughts, ideas, beliefs, and plans. There were pretty severe limits on "extracurricular" pursuits on campus, however. My mother made the comment that I was suspected of taking the study course by the Braille method.

The Late Night Swim

There were a couple of bars not far from the college, across the state line in New York, where the drinking age was only 18. The State Line Club actually straddled the line, with a moving bar that at one time could be rolled from one state to the other, depending on which State authority was threatening. A bit further down the highway there was a more attractive hangout for college kids, with a good piano player who always signed off a set with, "I'll be back in a flash with more trash for your cash!"

We liked that place, where discussions ranged from books to romance to philosophy, and lasted into the wee hours. After one evening so engaged, we were driving home and decided to stop at a place called "The Tubs," a natural water slide, owned by a cranky farmer, and thus only visited at night. We were undeterred by the lack of bathing suits or towels; foresight wasn't a strong suit for people our age. After a refreshing romp sliding over the smooth falls into the cool water, we figured it wouldn't be a good idea to return to the college in soaking wet clothes and drove on in our undies.

To our surprise, when we got to the Vermont state line, there was a drunk check under way, headed by the D.A. from Bennington. There was no possibility of escape and it looked like we were doomed. We stopped, the D.A. poked his big police flashlight through the window and looked at these two bedraggled kids with water flowing down their faces, not exactly dressed for church. Even worse, he immediately recognized me as Doc Browning's kid, paused, then mercifully said "Get out of here!" I figured things would get better, but when we got to my house for towels and dry clothes, my mother was standing in the upstairs bedroom window, watching us sashay across the lawn.

The trips to and from the college were taxing in other ways. There was some kind of industrial plant at a curve along the road to town. One night, returning home in my father's Buick convertible, I dozed off, and the car cut across an S curve, clipping off the 4 x 4 post holding up a traffic sign. This did not bode well. I got home, and found the damage was limited, bending the chrome bumper back against the tire. As I attempted to straighten it with a pry bar, it suddenly popped back into normal position, to my great astonishment and relief. Later at breakfast I mentioned it to my father, who only responded, "That's a good thing, since I sold the car last night." It was nice to be out of trouble, but also disheartening, since I had dreamed of buying that car from Dad when I graduated from college.

The tumultuous romantic times ended abruptly during Christmas of the senior year. I was taking an independent study course which required caring for the lab animals at Dartmouth during Christmas break.

My lady friend drove up from Boston, and it looked like an ideal time to be together at the deserted fraternity house. However, after driving all that way in bad weather to see me, she inexplicably turned around and left, and I never saw her again. She did return the engagement emerald earrings, which George Fenzl and I wore as tie tacks for a number of years, until my wife Sadako claimed them for a custom ring she wanted.

I think we remember our favorite professors and friends more than the books. The first time I met George, he appeared in my ground floor dorm room one morning, having climbed through the window of our basement room and slept on the couch. (It did seem odd that most of my acquaintances arrived through windows.) He was a frequent visitor after that, except for a short time when he was on probation after he passed out climbing the stairs to his dorm room. The campus chief of police carried him up the last flight of stairs to that room in his dorm. George's father ran an auto repair business in Philadelphia and drove to Hanover when there were car problems at Dartmouth, which were frequent with our cars at that time. George had an ancient Hudson four-door, which we often drove to Bennington to see my folks or visit the girls at Bennington College. On one trip, after we had driven at breakneck speeds for 100 miles on 2-lane Vermont roads and just arrived in Bennington, the right front suspension failed, dumping the car into a neighbor's yard. Thinking back to that trip around the curves on Old Highway 7, I shuddered a bit. Another "Shoulda been dead."

Another not-so-well thought out plan involved fraternity hazing. One night, one of our brothers was kidnaped by upper classmen, which usually resulted in a cold walk home. We borrowed a vehicle from another upperclassman friend in the dorm and gave chase.

The car was low on gas, the usual state of affairs for college students. To deal with this, I figured we could follow the kidnappers with the headlights off, and perhaps they would think they had lost us and drop off our mate so we could pick him up. Unfortunately, there was an S-turn in the road crossing a small brook. In the darkness, we missed the turn, and ended up crashing into small trees in the woods on the riverbank. Nothing was hurt except our wallets, and the difficulty explaining the whole thing to the owner of the car.

John Baldwin, the third of our dauntless trio shared study rooms at the fraternity junior and senior year. He had a Chevy sedan and was a .30-06 deer hunter. Sometimes, late in the evening we would pile in the car and hunt for rats at the dump in the nearby town of Lebanon with the .30-06 and a flashlight. That may have been the most vermin-free dump in New England!

One weekend, John returned from the New Hampshire woods with a 234-pound deer strapped to the fender of his Chevy. Either due to poor lighting or alcohol, George spied the deer, took aim with the .30-06 and fortunately missed the deer and the car, but blew a hole in the maple tree behind it sufficient to start sap flowing early.

My roommate, George, also had an old breech loading shotgun. One night, in mock anger at the guys at the other end of the hall he shoved a giant gumdrop into the gun, followed by a large firecracker, which he lit and quickly closed the breech. His aim wasn't all that bad, and the gumdrop hit the wall at the end of the hall dead center with enough force to fracture the plaster. The lady who kept the house clean was also the unofficial house mother. She also owned the freezer storage company holding our venison for clandestine meals, and sometimes let us use her cabin in the woods. She took a dim view of these shenanigans; don't know whether she took the repairs out of his wallet or his hide.

Perhaps the most remarkable survival occurred when George decided he was going to Bennington alone and slipped away. He made it down the highway about 30 miles, where he fell asleep, ran off the road, and crashed into a house being moved, which was up on 8 x 8 beams, 30 yards off the road. The whole house collapsed on him, and he reported waking up in the blackness, saying "Oh shit, I'm dead." Then later waking again, saying "Oh, shit, I'm not dead!" I don't remember how we rescued him, nor what happened to the house or the car, but he did say years later that there was still a warrant out for him in Vermont.

Another winter night, fueled with alcohol, my roommate again decided to borrow a car to drive to Bennington. A fist fight ensued on the icy driveway when I refused to turn over the keys, and between ice and alcohol, he ended up with a broken nose, so we went to Bennington anyway so my father could set the fracture in the middle of the night, while I endured my mother's wrath for "hurting my best friend."

One spring afternoon, we were driving to Bennington when we got onto some glare ice from snow melt run-off at a nearby ski resort. The car began a slow spin with absolutely no response to the steering wheel as we approached an S-curve crossing a railroad track on a downgrade. I had visions of the car striking the tracks sideways and cartwheeling into the ravine on the downhill side. We could only look at each other as the car continued the slow rotation until it was aligned with the rail crossing on dry concrete, and we proceeded on our way. Another "Shoulda been dead."

George's parents gave him a brand-new Ford convertible for graduation. At the end of our time at Dartmouth, George and I drove to Pensacola for Navy flight training and happy days followed. Innocents, we tried to drive through the main gate to the Naval Air Station, and handed our orders to the Marine sentry, whose only response was, "One Ford, going 'round!" Deflated, we exited, to return the next day with better results.

George at Commissioning

Because I became an Ensign on graduation from College, I could eat in the officers' club, have a car on base, and have an easier time with the physical training requirement. At Dartmouth, George had not been in the NROTC program, so he entered the Navy as a Naval Cadet, or NavCad, and had none of the privileges of an

A dashing officer and gentleman!

officer. He couldn't use his car until he was commissioned a few months later. Thus I "had" to keep his car for him.

One day, as his platoon was jogging along the dusty road in the hot sun out to the obstacle course, a car full of Ensigns in his car passed them on the way to the course, with me at the wheel. He still regales listeners with that story.

New Orleans

During ground school in Pensacola, we decided to drive to New Orleans over Labor Day. After checking in at a hotel on Canal Street, and making the rounds, we headed to a very old and fancy restaurant named Antoine's, which my mother had recommended.

The menu and wine list were entirely in French, with no prices listed. Neither of us spoke French and it fell to George to order the wine. Lacking help from the snooty waiter, he pointed to a line on the wine menu. The waiter brought the bottle, which looked like it had survived the French Revolution, and served him a taste. After going through the motions, George stood up and spit it on the carpet, saying "That's terrible!" Thus, we escaped the astronomical price of a mystery bottle of French wine and found a more hospitable place for dinner.

The next day, after touring Bourbon Street, and the Café du Monde where they served New Orleans coffee and the delicious beignets (better than a doughnut), we found a more reasonable restaurant, followed by bar hopping. I became enamored with a girl in one bar, and followed her to the next, but then found out from the bartender she was also in hot pursuit of her next boyfriend who was gay.

George had a short arm cast for a fracture sustained during a NavCad boxing match. When an overly friendly man next to him said in a sweet voice, "Hey, fella, how did you get that injury?" George responded, "Some guy made a pass at my girlfriend, and I decked him!" The man quickly lost interest and sidled away.

Eventually, George headed back to the hotel since we were running out of money while I enjoyed the end of someone's Chinese wedding reception at another bar.

Gazing at the Mississippi River from the end of Canal Street at around 4:00 a.m. there was an undeniable urge to go for a swim. I folded up my clothes, watch, and wallet in a neat bundle and dove in. In the darkness the dive was from a greater height than it looked, and I nearly lost my shorts, but did make it across the river. The area across the river belonged to the military, as manned by a guard with a carbine who informed me there was "No Trespassing."

By now it was dawn, I was sober, and the downstream current made it difficult to figure out where my clothes were, Amazingly, a voice from a Chris Craft pleasure boat came across the water, "You need a lift?" I think I answered that I wasn't properly dressed. He sent his daughter below and took me on board, and returned to the only available landing nearby, which turned out to be the gangplank of a Navy ship. By this time, people were lining up to take the ferry across the river, watching this play out.

When I got back to my neatly folded clothes, there was a greeting party -- a police car, a motorcycle cop, and an ambulance. They promptly took me into custody for "attempted suicide." The only way out of that mess was to retrieve my Navy swimming card proving I could swim a mile. At that point they were happy to turn me over to the military police, where I faced a very helpful Master Sargent. My clothes were soaked, and water was dripping on the floor, but I remember he kept asking me to stand at ease. When he found that the media had collected outside, he arranged for me to be taken back to our hotel via an underground exit, avoiding the news people.

George was not amused, and we quickly packed and fled the city, listening to brief news clips about the "Navy man celebrating the holiday." When my commanding officer got the report from the M.P.s, he seemed to lack a sense of humor, lumping me with all sorts of derelicts, criminals, and miscreants.

Flight Training

After finishing ground school, we moved through the stages of flight training – 80 hours in the old SNJ (North American T-6 Texan) at Whiting Field, formation and night flying and navigation at Saufley Field, and field practice carrier landings at outlying grass fields in Alabama, since carrier qualification was required for all Navy and Marine pilots to get the wings of gold.

A carrier approach to the ship had to be made at near-stall speed in order to catch one of the heavy cables strung across the flight deck. If one banked too much, the stall speed increased, and the airplane went into a low altitude spin leading to a (usually life ending) crash. One guy in our class had a stall-spin into the pine trees on a practice approach but was able to recover just in time to level and clip two trees. Hours later I saw him in the mess hall, still beyond pale!

Later, as a squadron safety officer, I had access to a report which showed a Naval Aviation mortality rate of 10 percent during those years.

After 150 hours of flight time and 170 landings, and clearance by the LSOs (Landing Signal Officers) monitoring our landings, we were ready to fly out to the USS Saipan, a straight deck carrier, in the Gulf of Mexico.

Most of us were pretty nervous at the prospect, but after the exhaustive training we robotically flew the pattern exactly as taught by our instructors. I remember nothing about the first approach after leaving the 180-degree position abeam the carrier until jerked to a stop after a successful arrested landing.

On the old straight deck carriers there was no option to "wave off" after cutting power, so a barrier was erected during flight operations between the landing aircraft and the airplanes parked forward. There was a movie clip of a jet which missed the wires, cartwheeled over the barrier into the mass of airplanes parked forward, with a resulting holocaust.

Trader Jon's

Flight training was not all study and terror – after all, the Gulf had wonderful beaches and, somehow, young (and not so young) ladies seemed to be attracted to the pilots. There was a bar in downtown Pensacola named Trader Jon's, probably remembered by everyone who ever got his or her Navy Wings.

It had a huge bar, with netting under the ceiling holding everything from airplane propellers to bras, contributed by generations of visitors. There was sawdust on the floor and the beer flowed freely. The waitresses were efficient, courteous, and untouchable. They carried the drink trays on their heads, and they always made it to the tables in an adjoining area for those with dates.

Sometimes high school kids in tuxedos and gowns would show up. One night we heard a ruckus above the usual din – it seems one of the high school girls objected to her date's admiration of the waitresses, climbed onto the table, and pulled off her gown. Jon instantly appeared from nowhere with a blanket and hustled her off to his office to call her parents.

Another night, as George and I were standing at the bar, a girl armed with a water pistol fired at him; he promptly wrestled her to the sawdust covered floor, and they tussled for the weapon until her date showed up with fist cocked. As George rose to meet him, the guy saw the Dartmouth logo on his windbreaker, and they started chatting amiably while the woman lay now abandoned in the sawdust.

Memory may be clouded as to time or location, but it seems that the transit of beer through the system was such that the restrooms were always crowded. There was a convenient wall along the side of the building, frequently used in a pinch. Jon didn't like that much, and there was a "sea story" that he had the metal wall electrified and the first few "shocked" males quickly passed the word, and all retreated indoors. I can't vouch for this paragraph!

Bikki and Jean

Sometimes things just turn out better than you expect. There was a very attractive girl from a wealthy family and a manicured ranch a bit north of Bennington. She went to private school and drove a Jaguar XK-120. She was absolutely out of my league during the high school years.

During the first Christmas leave during flight training my sister invited me to a party at the church in Old Bennington. Lo and behold, the Jaguar girl, Bikki, was there and told me to ditch the party and head elsewhere with her.

We retired to a bar, chatted over drinks, and to my surprise she joined us in Pensacola after New Year's, along with a friend, Jean, her parents had designated as chaperone.

The girls found a cottage near the Base on the Gulf, and George and I spent most of our time with them when we weren't flying. The girls did have a more noble purpose than flirting with budding aviators, since they both had snagged jobs with the Girl Scouts in Dallas and departed when we were transferred to another base.

We then agreed to get together in New Orleans for Easter, and the girls took the train from Dallas and joined us for the long weekend. The girls elected separate rooms at our hotel on Canal Street, and we enjoyed their company, took in good restaurants and those delicious beignets with chicory laced coffee at the Café Du Monde.

Bikki and the Buick.

Bikki agreed to join me for Easter services at the Episcopal Cathedral, although she was Jewish, and we left our roommates sleeping. It might have been the lack of breakfast, or protestant incense, but Bikki had a sinking spell, and ended up lying in the back pew for the rest of the service. We returned to the hotel, to find the other two together in bed! So much for the chaperone idea.

We were usually behind schedule, and when the girls had to return to Dallas, they nearly missed the train. One of the girls made it, but lost a shoe trying to get on the moving train. The road ran next to the tracks for a long way, and we pursued the train to its next stop, where shoes, baggage, and girls were reunited.

ADVANCED TRAINING

After finishing basic, formation, navigation, and carrier qualification, we finally got into "big boy" airplanes, first the T-28 Trojan with more power and advanced navigation equipment and had more night flying. After that the next duty station was Memphis, where we got introduced to jets in the Lockheed T-33, a straight-wing plane with large wingtip fuel tanks, a version of which was first used in combat in the Korean war.

The training included the art of formation flying, which was quite different in jets, with no big prop to slow the aircraft if you "join up" with the leader a bit fast. Perhaps the most important thing learned in this transition was the importance of fuel management for those thirsty engines.

In Memphis there were new friendships. One fellow trainee, also named Bill, became a close friend. He was an interesting guy who, among other things, had bought an old hearse during his college years in the Midwest, and parlayed that into a partnership in a gospel funeral home. He also was a scientist and a mathematician with many innovative ideas.

He owned a sleek new Chrysler, with "The Highway Hi-Fi Record Player," which was one of the earliest music players. We thought we were "cool" until a car full of young girls next to us stopped at a light, and we heard them disdainfully say, "Oh they're old." We were 22.

At the time, the movie *Carmen Jones* was playing at a Memphis drive-in. The movie was an adaptation of the opera *Carmen*, and everyone in the cast was African American.

Bill and I were completely innocent of the issues of segregation, and when we drove in and bought our tickets, the manager immediately came to our car, pointed out we weren't supposed to be there, but satisfied we weren't looking for trouble, told us to park next to the projection room, and not get out of the car. The movie was excellent, and we survived without incident or trips to the rest room.

From Memphis our class transferred to Corpus Christi on the Gulf in Texas for the final phase of advanced training in operational jets (at that time the F9F Panther, a wonderful Grumman plane). Gunnery training was the best part of that, and our flight of four set a new record against the banner pulled by another Panther. There was a tendency to get fixated on the target, and if you continued to turn toward the banner, you would be lined up on the tow plane. The instructor flying the tow plane didn't favor that at all.

F9F Panther.

Flight School Graduation

Finally, 15 months after we started in Pensacola, we lined up in pressed uniforms, to pin on our "Wings of Gold." My sister came from Chicago to do the honors for me.

My sister, Suzie, and me.

Bill Joyce, the buddy in Memphis, graduated at the same time, and we decided to drive to Monterrey, Mexico, for the Labor Day weekend before leaving the area. We were joined by a good friend, a female Naval Officer who lived in the same quarters area, and we often had dinner together. The trip we had planned turned out to be quite different than expected. All hotels in Monterrey were sold out, and the restaurants were full. We ended up sleeping in an open pasture; the girls got the car, and we slept on the grass. I woke up to see a cow nearly standing over Bill, who was still asleep. To use a bad pun, we decided to seek greener pastures, and drove up into the mountains to a small village called Saltillo. At some point we were passed on the highway by two men on a motorcycle, both toting long guns. That gave us pause. The town was home to silver artisans and zapateros who hand-crafted boots. I bought a pair which were 'almost' regulation, except for the zippers, and the girls collected jewelry. The hotel/motel where we stayed was owned by an expatriate Navy Chief. At that time there was a gondola which ascended the mountain for a view of the surrounding country. A nice place and nice people. The current Google pictures are certainly different from the dusty roads and single service station we found in 1956!

Since all four of us were from the Midwest or New England, we all headed home together. We parted from Bill Joyce at his home and continued to Vermont in the Buick. After a short visit with Mom and Dad, we then headed west, with stops at Niagara Falls. My sister and my Navy friend were left in Chicago, and I headed for San Diego. The road west was lonely, but pleasant, through New Mexico and Arizona.

Sister Suzie (right) in Saltillo, Mexico.

Hitchhiking was more common in those days, and an old prospector joined me for a while in the desert. He was a remarkable man, hunting for uranium and silver, with a knowledge of where to find water in the desert, and stories about the old Tex-Mex railroad which wandered back and forth over the southern border without problems.

Brown Field and VU-3

Most of us aspired to assignment in a jet fighter squadron, but at that time the first squadron assignment had nothing to do with one's prowess in flight training, setting a new gunnery record, or satisfactory carrier landings. It depended on the needs of varied squadrons. Those of us in my class were sent to multi-engine, transport, or utility squadrons. Arriving at Brown Field in San Diego I was taken aback a bit by the sight of lines of WWII F6F Hellcats, painted red and looking like something left over from WWII.

Even without the aid of iPhone or GPS, finding Brown Field in San Diego wasn't much of a challenge. On the road between the field and the bay, there was only one yellow stop light.

There was another odd-looking aircraft standing on its tail near the runway. We found out it was an experimental vertical take-off airplane called the "Pogo." Never saw it move from its tether, however. Never seen one since.

The Pogo.

Checking in at the duty office, getting assigned to the BOQ (bachelor officer quarters), and finding the chow hall was easy since everything was next to the one runway. Some remnants of the squadron buildings are still there.

My roommate was a wild man, who arduously worked to lead me astray for three years. He was a very good pilot, great friend, and, eventually, was best man at our wedding in Okinawa.

His treatment for a hangover was breakfast across the border in Tijuana. It certainly was a bargain at $1.25 for great steak and eggs or rabbit and eggs and good coffee. The only downside was getting back across the border, even back then. We usually were greeted by the Feds with a leer, and "Well, have a good night, boys?" When the response was that we just came down for breakfast, it became "All Right – out of the car!" They even removed the air vents in the Buick, looking for contraband or drugs.

The flying was interesting, if not glamorous. The red Hellcats were configured for drone radio control with old vacuum tube systems which weren't very reliable. The yellow and blue ones had a little control box on the canopy rail for guiding the drones while flying one's own aircraft.

A senior controller would stand on the runway with his little control box and launch the drone, following which we would join up and guide it out to sea, for a ship's gunnery practice.

Because of the fragility of the old control systems, three control planes were standard, call-signs Charlie One, Two, and Three. If we lost control of the drone, either due to electronic failure or flak damage, it had to be shot down before it could stray over any populated areas. I think I hold the record for an American pilot shooting down the most American airplanes – a dubious honor.

F6Fs being transferred to Alameda
for shipment to Okinawa.

The different colored aircraft, red for targets and blue for controllers, was supposed to make it clear where to shoot but sometimes our shipboard colleagues didn't get the distinction, and one control plane came back with a bunch of holes in the airplane's fuselage and canopy and a disturbed pilot.

There was a news clip when the radio control of one of our drones was lost, after which it overflew a number of populated areas including San Diego and parts of Los Angeles. The Air Force, anxious for the practice, had F-89 squadrons on standby to shoot down errant drones but, in this case, they were not successful, although they did start a few brush fires along the way. The drone eventually ran out of fuel and crashed somewhere up in the mountains.

We also had the job of towing banners like the airplanes you may see advertising off the beach, but ours were towed for gunnery practice. The banner was to be dropped beside the runway before landing. For some reason, one of my colleagues didn't or couldn't release the banner, and came in a bit low on the approach, snagging the border fence, dragging it onto the runway. That effectively shut down flight operations for the day!

Juveniles

During our time at VU-3 in San Diego, we were required to maintain night flying proficiency. Somebody had the not-so-bright idea of going up to the Cajon Pass area to have fun with the freight trains. There used to be a steep descent into San Bernardino, with multiple turns to reduce the grade, including a 360-degree circle, although there is no trace of that on modern maps.

The trick was to find a train coming down the mountain and then line up heading toward the oncoming train, with all lights off. The landing light was turned on as the train came closer, with the expected result being sparks when the engineer applied emergency brakes due to the illusion that a train was coming up the grade on the same track in the opposite direction.

As a disclaimer, we were most definitely not involved in a derailment which occurred much later when two trains collided in the city.

Junior officers in those days were not what you would call wealthy, and Christmas was coming soon. My roommate connected me with a pottery shop in Chula Vista which had classes in making decorative cups and plates.

Casting the plates, cups, and saucers was fun, and hand painting with a unique decoration for each family member was even more so. There was the time pressure to get the items done by Christmas. The lady who owned the shop and did the teaching gave me keys to work nights and weekends.

She was married to a senior commander at a nearby base but had a wandering eye. Toward the end, there was quite a bit of time spent circling the tables in the shop. I think the modern term for these ladies is a "cougar." Her kindness included sending her Commander husband in to deliver Sunday dinner to a very uncomfortable Ensign!

When the set of dishes was packed up and the eight place-settings were finished, the lady gave me something for a headache, and as I headed up the hill to Brown Field, I was overtaken by dizziness and double vision. I reported to the base dispensary and said I thought I had been poisoned. Without a second glance, the corpsman on duty said, "If it doesn't get better, come back in the morning."

The LaGuardia Caper

Large military bases often have "space available" on transport flights, and the opportunity to fly home to Vermont for Christmas in 1956 arose. A Marine pilot was ferrying a T-33 from San Diego to New York at the perfect time. When I met him at North Island and offered to help with navigation, his response was "Do you want a ride or don't you?" Thus chastened, I picked up the parachute and my gear, loaded it in the back seat, and we left NAS North Island a few days before Christmas.

He planned to navigate all the way to New York using tactical air navigation (TACAN) only. TACAN was an advanced system for that time, providing both direction and distance to the next point on the route. His arrogance and poor planning soon got him into trouble when the TACAN transponder failed before we got to Colorado, since he had no charts or other navigation aids.

He declared an emergency when, and in spite of help from ground controllers, he mistook Colorado Springs for NAS Denver and had to declare a second emergency to get to the Navy Base. The command duty officer at the Naval Air Station took a dim view of his performance and he was summarily relieved of the airplane, and I was relieved of my transportation.

I was able to catch a ride on an Air Force cargo plane headed to Pease AFB in New Hampshire. We landed safely in very icy weather and Dad picked me up for a nice Christmas at home.

I still had uniforms and a very heavy parachute, complete with a raft in the seat pack of the chute, facing the prospect of flying commercial out of LaGuardia in New York. After a significant New Year's Eve celebration in New York City with friends, I got to the American Airlines ticket counter in dress blues, Navy overcoat, and the parachute, which made my baggage a lot overweight. Perhaps the agent wasn't thrilled with working New Year's Eve, and gruffly told me it would be $75 extra for the parachute. Filled with yule spirits and a bit of alcohol, my exact response was "O.K., I'll wear it!"

Trudging out across the wet tarmac toward the airplane wearing the parachute, a number of civilians began to slow down a bit, perhaps wondering why a Navy pilot would see the need for a parachute on their flight. The airline personnel were perhaps even more concerned about the image, and belatedly an agent chased me down with the news that they had found a government regulation which allowed them to carry government equipment with no charge. Problem solved, I smiled and had a nice flight back to San Diego!

The Nob Hill Gang

The attrition for our F6F target planes was high due to operational losses and, at one point, we were charged with delivering 13 drones in one flight to Alameda for shipment to Okinawa. This led to the choice of a lot of junior pilots taking airplanes without navigation gear, and flying in formation with a P2V, which was a large antisubmarine aircraft with good navigation capability. The formation wasn't particularly "tight" on the way north, but we all got lined up in echelon on the P2V for landing at Alameda. Surprisingly, the group of 13 airplanes in echelon looked pretty good as we approached the field.

However, the P2V mistook Oakland Airport for Alameda, and made a sudden corrective turn into the echelon. Turning into the echelon is a big no-no at any time, but with 13 aircraft piloted by juniors on your wing, was a real disaster! I was somewhere in the middle of the gaggle and watched with horror as the first Hellcat cut power dramatically, the second dropped his landing gear to slow down, the third deployed both gear and flaps, and the rest scattered like ducks in hunting season. It must have been a glorious sight from the ground for everyone except the tower controllers!

While we all were awaiting transportation back to San Diego, someone mentioned he knew some girls, stewardesses who shared a large apartment on Nob Hill in San Francisco. Navy pilots were more welcome than Air Force guys since we brought our own booze. The girls renting the apartment were rotating onto flights all the time, so the party became sort of a permanent arrangement.

Somehow, I found myself chatting with a lady the others called "Fat Pat" when she wasn't within hearing distance. I mercifully escaped with the flight back to San Diego, but the party apparently continued. "Pat" somehow got a line on my college roommate George and followed him to his BOQ at Alameda. According to him, the pursuit extended to his room, into the adjoining room, and out the second story window, where his fall was mercifully broken by a pine tree, following which he locked himself in the trunk of his car until she tired of the hunt!

Thoughts on Vietnam

My awareness of Vietnam developed in '55 or '56, chatting with Ted Miller, a Navy intelligence officer for whom I was later best man. He had been stationed in Saigon back when the French were still in charge. His assessment was that the French should leave, but that we should not replace them.

Most of the pilots I knew called it "McNamara's War" and were less than enthusiastic. Part of that was due to the civilian intervention in every detail. Pilots couldn't drop bombs if it was cloudy in Hanoi. No missions when kids were going to school or returning home. No bombing dams, since damaging the rice crops might make people go hungry. No night raids. The route to target was mandated to avoid overflight of schools, embassies, and a million other limitations on the way in. From a survival point of view, flying in low would get you shot down by anti-aircraft fire. Flying too high would get you shot down by a surface to air (SAM) missile, so entry and exit was actually a narrow tube. The pilots used to joke that if you were Vietnamese, you didn't need to know how to shoot. After breakfast, just man the guns, and wait for the Americans to come down the narrow corridor.

When George was skipper of a squadron whose mission was to suppress anti-aircraft flak, they had flown to Hanoi from the carrier and finding it overcast had to head back. You couldn't land on the carrier with unexpended ordinance, and there was a hamlet along the way where there was anti-aircraft fire every time they passed by. George decided to take a look, since the weather was clear in that area. As they rolled into a dive to end that, they spotted a lone man a short distance from the town on old manual 27mm antiaircraft gun.

As they dove, he jumped off the gun and was frantically pedaling his old bicycle down the road toward home. Nobody had the heart to shoot at him and they dumped the explosives into the ocean on the way back to the ship.

George denies the following, but there is fairly clear recollection of events as related to me. While on an earlier deployment, he had a "soft" cat shot, (too little acceleration) and went off the end, didn't hit the water, but sank into ground effect until he burned off enough fuel and was able to climb.

That led to thoughts about career direction and troubles at home with the result that he turned in his wings to the air boss on the ship, who took him off flight status, but made him mull it over during the deployment. After some time of "watching," and not "doing," he decided to return to flying.

There was a hold-back grip for keeping the throttle at full power during the jolt of a catapult shot. On his first launch, the throttle hold back broke loose, and he again cleared the deck with the engine in idle, and flew in ground effect again, barely off the water. It appears the decision was "whatever will be, will be!"

The stay at Brown Field after Christmas was brief. The Utility Squadrons had detachments in Hawaii, Okinawa, and Japan. A squadron junior pilot in Okinawa got killed doing unauthorized acrobatics at low altitude.

The Navy wanted a replacement in 24 hours, so I packed most of my worldly possessions into a duffel bag, with the rest going into the trunk of the Buick, which was left at Brown Field.

It remained neglected there for months until authorization for shipment of vehicles to Okinawa was received. My friend George was rooming at Alameda with Ted Miller, the intelligence officer from Saigon.

Ted agreed to drive the Buick from San Diego to Alameda for trans-shipment. It seemed like it would be a joy ride, but the car had suffered badly from the exposure time at Brown Field. George gave me a hilarious account of Ted's trip. Shortly after he got on the highway, the radiator overheated. Simple, right? Remove the thermostat. He got out in the rain with his wrenches and was more than dismayed to find it had already been removed sometime in the past! Then the aging convertible top started to shred, and he arrived soaked, cold, angry, and threw the keys on George's desk with appropriate comments. I guess the friendship survived, since I was later asked to be best man at his wedding.

After being flown to Alameda, I joined Lt Cdr. Bolar, who would become the new Officer in Charge at the detachment in Okinawa. When we arrived in Tokyo, we parted ways in the part of Tokyo known as the Ginza, either because he had business at NAS Atsugi, or he got lost in the "Ville." I had only a vague idea of where the military base was but walking 5 or 10 miles west through Tokyo after midnight proved quite safe, until the arrival of a taxi seemed like an even better idea.

OKINAWA

Our detachment in Okinawa was based at a large joint use airfield in the capital city of Naha, at the site of the Japanese fighter base during the war. With two Air Force F-86s ready to scramble at any time, as well as a Navy Patrol Squadron, with some Chinese commercial aircraft landing the wrong way on the single runway, life was "interesting."

Our "poor cousin" detachment was relegated to a Quonset hut, with 20 to 40 F6F Hellcat drones and control planes parked in front.

When new red airplanes were shipped from the U.S., we were required to put ten hours on the autopilot before the airplane could be launched as a NOLO (no live operator) on an actual operation. That was fairly dull flying, sitting there on autopilot, but it did provide opportunities to enjoy the view and take pictures of this beautiful 70-mile-long island.

F6F flight line at Naha.

Drone service to the fleet called for three control planes and a (piloted) drone to fly across the island and land at Yonabaru, a deserted Japanese air strip in the midst of sugar cane fields. Our mobile control truck, a fire truck, an ambulance, and a gas truck would follow us. The runway was close to the shore of Buckner Bay, and not very close to populated areas, which was good for everyone involved.

After getting set up, the pilot of the selected drone aircraft would lock the brakes, and leave the aircraft, which would then be controlled from the ground during take-off, then passed to the lead control plane, also a Hellcat.

As mentioned, the targets were left-over F6F Hellcat planes from WWII, reconfigured to be controlled by the pilot or another airplane. The electronics were not very dependable; thus the need for a control plane and two back-ups. The control planes were also Hellcats, with a yellow and blue paint scheme, which hopefully would deter shipboard gunners from shooting at them. This blue and yellow paint scheme was mostly successful, although one control plane came back with bullet holes from just behind the cockpit all the way back to the tail! The pilot was able to fly it back to Okinawa, but it had to be junked after landing, due to the battle damage.

A "good" drone landing after gunfire damage.

The assignment had some exciting moments; 25 percent of the drones crashed on take-off or landing and 25 percent were shot down, so anytime there was a drone operation, one had a 50 percent chance of seeing an airplane wreck.

Interacting with the surrounding farmers was interesting as well, since they tended to salvage anything that wasn't tied down. After one wreck which left a magnesium engine cylinder on fire, a farmer scooped it up in his straw hat and dunked it in the water in the ditch next to the runway. When it came out of the water, still burning, he was dumbfounded and just watched it burn through his conical straw hat. One time the resourceful villagers tried to reclaim some of the runway by dumping dirt on it and planting crops. We discouraged that since the unmanned airplanes sometimes got away on launch or ended up on fire on the runway or in the adjoining fields.

Despite the checkout and previous testing, sometimes the drones "got away," either because the electronics failed or there was battle damage caused by the ships. One time the pilots lost control of a drone, which then started flying random acrobatics over the ship. The folks on the ship were enthusiastic about the show until we told them we had no control over the plane, at which point every gun on the ship opened up!

Lt Cdr. Bolar was an excellent ground controller and martini drinker – he won a bet that he could launch a live drone with a bag over his head and succeeded! Fortunately, those pictures never made it up the chain of command. His leadership style was to have three martinis (which became his nickname), then restrict the junior officers to the base for the night, since he didn't bother to become acquainted with the local people and didn't think we should be let loose in "town." Naha at that time was actually a city the same size as San Francisco.

The Great Target Island Caper of 1957

Due to the tenuous nature of maintaining control of the drones, the control planes were armed with six 50-caliber machine guns and had periodic gunnery proficiency training in case a drone had to be shot down before it endangered the ship or people on the ground.

There was a U.S. military target island 50 miles west of Okinawa with a bullseye painted in the middle for bombing practice. It also had multiple warning signs in several languages, The boss, perhaps afflicted by a little "senior vision," led our flight of four out to the target island for our practice.

We circled the target area and he said he was picking out a small tree as a target on the beach, and rolled in, saying, "Follow Me!" Late in the dive he suddenly shouted, "Cease fire, cease fire!" It turned out that the "tree" was a man, who sprinted away as he saw the bullets raking the sand. Fortunately, he wasn't hit since three of the six guns on the boss's airplane jammed. We returned to base and got a helicopter to take us out to ensure the man wasn't injured.

We first landed at the target area and found a garden planted in the middle of the bullseye! There was a village on a nearby island. With the aid of a translator, we had a "conference" with the mayor or leader of the group about the dangers on the target island. After emphasizing the risks inherent in trespassing, our leader asked about the garden in the middle of the bullseye, to which the answer was, "That's the safest place. Nobody ever hits that!" So much for the effort at diplomacy.

To top off a bad day on the job, the helicopter in which we were passengers developed a red transmission warning light, which was never a good thing in a helicopter 50 miles at sea. That is probably the reason that most sane pilots insist on having two wings when they leave the ground.

The Bullet Head

The most junior pilot (Bullet) in our little group was disliked by all, and he probably reciprocated. When we were out with a drone on a live exercise, he was always tail-end Charlie and sometimes wandered off looking for whales, instead of staying in formation. He was also forever complaining that he never got to shoot down a drone if we lost control of it. On one of these occasions, we did lose control of the drone and I was closing on it to shoot it down when suddenly there were 50 caliber tracers zipping by on both sides of me! Thankfully the six machine guns were calibrated to converge at 1000 yards, and I did a quick barrel roll and ended up behind him, with a powerful urge to let off a burst.

He did not like Okinawa, Okinawan people, or much of anything else. He also felt that married guys got favored treatment when shipping household goods back to the States and said he was shipping 3000 pounds of bricks to get even. He always sported a buzz cut and looked a bit like a WWII storm trooper. As a proud Iowan beer drinker, he sneered at us "Ivy League" boys until he lost his first chug-a-lug contest to one of us.

During a typhoon, he ran out into the storm, and nearly garroted himself on the steel clothesline outside the barracks. He was left lying in a deep puddle in the rain. Once we were sure he was breathing, we just stood around and watched.

Another interesting guy was a cool Marine Warrant Officer assigned to the base. "Gunny," as we called him, was also the Marine Corps Champion handball player at the time. He would take on three of us in a 21-point game, give us a 19-point lead, and still regularly beat us. Gunny used to enjoy a blistering serve. His favorite was to hit Bullet directly on the back of his skull, causing a huge spray of sweat to fly up in the air from his Nazi-style crew cut.

Too Low

There were some close calls. One of our jobs was to provide training for the ships against torpedo or strafing attacks. While the sailors manned the guns to practice target acquisition (and hopefully not fire) our two- or four-plane formations simulated the attack.

This exercise was designed with torpedo runs at low altitude and from different directions to teach the crew on the ship about tracking aircraft skimming the water. The seas were quite choppy that day, enough for some sea spray. With my roommate on my wing, we turned in for the run and something went quite wrong. Either there was a rogue wave, or the spray shorted out the old electric shackles on the external belly tank, turning it into a giant speed brake, or I was just cutting it too close.

Approaching the ship at 250 knots, suddenly there was a jolt, and the propeller suddenly came to a stop bent oddly at a 90° angle against the cowling. I radioed to my wingman, "I'm going in!" Apparently he didn't get the gravity of the situation and replied, "Roger, right behind you!" I kidded him (much) later about that. Fortunately, the airplane skipped like a flat rock, gliding to a pancake landing rather than digging in, which probably would have been fatal. It came to rest, nose down, sinking fast, not more than 100 yards from the ship. A rapid exit from the aircraft followed, although the chute deployed in the wind, threatening to drag me under. The ship maneuvered to pick me up directly without having to launch a small boat and cut loose the parachute. Another "Shoulda been dead."

At that point, the exercise was halted, and the ship returned to the pier while I pondered my fate. We had a new skipper, but he and his wife were on leave in Hong Kong at the time. Since I was flying "his" airplane that day, I wondered how to break it to him when he returned. Back at home base, the squadron didn't help my cause much, having planted a little cross where the boss's airplane was supposed to be parked.

RIP!

Typhoon

We had extensive exposure to typhoons. During one we had 12 inches of rain in 12 hours, and 24 inches in 36 hours. The BOQ (bachelor officer quarters) was on a hill overlooking the airfield and the sea, and we watched parts of Quonset huts blowing across the fields.

Before one storm, a flight of Marine A-1 fighters flew in from Japan. The A-1, or AD as it was known then, was a big brother to our Hellcats. Since there was no hangar space for our old aircraft during typhoons, we used a nine-point tie-down (nine separate ropes securing the airplane) and while the paint might be scrubbed off in the storm, the planes survived.

We offered help to the Marines, but they declined, and at first were even considering the crazy idea of setting up a bivouac near the runway. They only used their usual 3-point tie-down, then moved to the Fighter Club to weather the storm. During Typhoon Condition One, the Club stayed open 24 hours, but once there, one could not leave during the storm. It was a tough choice – snacks and beer in the BOQ or remain at the Fighter Club to party for the duration of the storm.

That storm was a big one, with maximum winds over the tower at 125 knots, or about 140 mph. When it was over, we went to survey the damage on the flight line. Our aircraft and Quonset office space were intact.

The Marine squadron with their 3-point tie-downs didn't do so well. All four planes had been ripped from their moorings and slid together like a deck of cards, coming to rest under the wing of a P2V patrol plane, which collapsed on top of the pile of planes. This led to a visit by a Marine General who wasn't pleased. The troops were somewhat subdued. I don't know whether he kicked them back to Iwakuni in Japan or loaded them in a plane for a lecture lasting the entire trip.

The Okinawan People

During our stay, the Okinawan people were hospitable, generous, and kind and, in general, the Navy enlisted men and junior officers responded in kind. On the other hand, the "official" U.S. stance was xenophobic. For example, "indigenous" people were not allowed to be guests in the officers' clubs. There was one civilian club where mixed couples were allowed as there was a significant civilian population of Americans, Filipinos, and Koreans at that time.

Many of the enlisted men moved into the "Ville," and rented nice little homes with their Okinawan girlfriends, many of whom they had met in the bars that lined the many streets in that part of the city. From our little detachment of 30 or 40 men, there were 10 who married Okinawans. At a reunion 10 years later, only one couple had ended up divorced at a time when the divorce rate in the U.S. was 50 percent. The chaplains handed out pamphlets to the young women suggesting they would be shunned, friendless, miserable, or deserted if they moved to the U.S. Interracial marriage was essentially impossible for officers. A predecessor of mine, another pilot, was forced to return to the U.S., get out of the Navy, and return as a civilian to marry his fiancée and claim their child. We still maintain contact with them and their five children.

Okinawan marketplace.

The harbor area also offered a lot of bars, some good little restaurants, and many clean, attractive homes. Most homes had city running water but usually not indoor bathrooms, so traditional bath houses were found in every neighborhood with separate facilities for men and women. Americans using the community baths got quizzical looks but were tolerated.

The Okinawan people were industrious and skilled at many things, including home building, boat building, tile and pottery, farming, and even glass blowing, with the limited equipment available at that time.

My future wife.

It had been only 10 years since the battle for Okinawa which cost the lives of over 100,000 civilians, and even worse casualties among the military on both sides. Remarkably, both in Okinawa and in Japan, we were never met with hostility or resentment. A squadron mate and I made a flight to Hiroshima, much of which was still being rebuilt. Even there, people were cordial and helpful to lost American tourists.

How I Met My Wife Sadako

When I arrived in Okinawa, my squadron mates were at the airport to greet me, including Bill Colohan, instigator of many adventures, and later my best man. The only reasonable option for eating on base was at the Fighter Club which had a gracious dining room and a very popular bar with cheap drinks subsidized by very loose slot machines. Okinawans staffed the kitchen, and diminutive Okinawan girls waited tables.

47

Shortly after my arrival there was a "theme night" party at the Fighter Club. That night it was the Old Wild West with a cowboy band. The waitresses were all wearing jeans and six shooters, which looked a bit strange on tiny Okinawan women. Serving our table was a girl commandeered from her usual job in the accounting office. She was quite shy, but later accepted a date to a movie with me.

That lady later became my wife. Our early dating nearly floundered due to the linguistic difficulty with "Tuesday" and "Thursday" which ended up with both of us waiting to meet the other on the wrong day, with obvious ruffled feelings. We eventually solved that mix-up, and Sadako and I continued to date. Her mother (Mrs. Uehara) spoke Okinawan and Japanese, but my skills were close to nil in both languages at the time.

Sadako was working to support her mother and four sisters, holding down two 8-hour jobs on base after the death of her father in 1946, so time for dating was limited. Introductions to the family were made, and eventual tentative approval of our dating ensued from Sadako's mother.

This eventually led to invitations for dinner at their home with classical Okinawan dances by her younger sisters, who were highly accomplished in that art. Meals might be Okinawan style, or Western style for holidays. Sadako's cousin enlisted me later to help with their remodeling jobs.

For a young Okinawan woman, it was a big risk to date an American; however, how innocent or casual that might be, most Okinawan families were quite opposed since the woman might have no option of marrying an Okinawan man later.

I think I only escaped that stigma because people joked that I was wooing her mother by fixing up things in their home.

Their home was tiny by American standards with a small cooking area, a formal living room, and two smaller sleeping rooms. At that time, the electric power company provided only one 40-watt light bulb fixture in the ceiling of the main room, which made it quite gloomy.

Since the PX on base carried all manner of things one might find Stateside, it was possible to find a two-tube industrial fluorescent light fixture and when I showed up with it one day, Mrs. Uehara allowed me to install it.

The improvement was quite remarkable. It certainly was the brightest living room in the community and became the focus of village interest and may even have led to some improvement in my prospects.

The next effort was not appreciated, however. Most homes had concrete block walls surrounding the yards, which were home to generations of cockroaches. It seemed an easy fix would be bug spray, but that didn't end well, since at the first blast of the aerosol, the resident roaches all fled to neighboring homes. One of Sadako's cousins taught me a lot about do-it-yourself, and even got me up on the roof helping to building a new house.

When Sadako could get off work we attended movies in Naha or had dinner dates at Castle Terrace, a civilian club which was the only option for people not allowed to dine at the military clubs to experience upscale dining.

The reason for that, I was told, was not prejudice, but necessity. It seems that the Air Force fighter pilots, previously on unaccompanied tours of duty, would bring the "girls" from town to the club. When theirs became a permanent assignment and families joined them, there was a significant problem when one of the ladies of the night showed up with a new date wandered to the table where the officer and his wife were dining, and casually asked, "How come you never come see me anymore?" This sometimes led to fireworks and an uncomfortable conversation between the flier and his wife.

A much more serious problem was related to the affairs between many of the pilots with Okinawan girlfriends, often half their age, leaving them with children and promising to return. The women only later found out that the father already had a wife and kids in the U.S.

That happened to our housemaid at the BOQ. She was an esteemed Geisha, and definitely not a prostitute. She got entangled with an American and ended up as our housemaid, with no prospects beyond that job. Sadako's senior manager at the club was also abandoned by the father of her child when he left. Thus it was, that most Okinawans looked on romantic relationships with Americans with strong disfavor for good reason.

Engagement

Sometime early in 1958, when we became more serious about the relationship, we started jumping through the extensive hoops required for military/civilian marriage, which were demeaning and obviously intended to prevent a marriage.

Once it occurred to my C.O. that the prospect of marriage seemed serious, I soon got orders back to Moffett Field near San Francisco. Fortunately, my C.O. at Moffett was a divorcee who also liked the fact that I was always ready to fly him to Los Angeles to see his girlfriend. He endorsed all the marriage forms without objection, and even let me go to Washington to hand carry documents required by the Pentagon. It was necessary to have permission from the local command in San Francisco to take more than 15 days leave. Permission from the command above that was needed to leave the United States. Permission was required from the command in Japan to visit their theater of operations, and to have an Army "Visa" from the Pentagon to visit Okinawa.

Many of the permissions had a specific time frame, and it could be "convenient" to make sure they did not overlap. One document needed signing at the Pentagon. It still brings a smile to remember quietly sitting in the office next to a signatory's desk at the Pentagon, with a bland expression while he tried to ignore me. He finally gave up in frustration, signed the papers and returned them to me with a snarl. That was fun.

My prospective wife certainly had the worst of it. She suffered the indignity of having to read a pamphlet at the chaplain's office clearly written for prostitutes, which pointed out how it would not be all "fun and games" in the U.S. with no Japanese friends, shunned by neighbors, etc.!

The most outrageous requirement was the medical evaluation, including three pelvic exams. She went to the dispensary at the Air Force Base, had the exam, was then told that it had to be done by a hospital-based doctor. After that, she was told that since she was marrying a Navy man, she had to be examined by a Navy doctor at a distant hospital! There were similar tactics at all the stops required for us to marry.

It seemed prudent to discuss the proposed marriage with my parents and, since my sister was graduating from Northwestern in the Chicago area, I flew to meet them to "discuss it," but then had to slip away with my sister to pick out a wedding ring. My distraught mother was stopped for erratic driving at 3:00 am, and a kindly policeman took her to an all-night diner for coffee and donuts to calm her down. My Dad may have feigned approval, but Mom later told me he was just as upset as she was.

In Okinawa, although we gained her mother's approval, most of the larger family was opposed. In addition, the U.S. Government was opposed to serious relationships with "indigenous people." Marriage between enlisted men and Okinawans was frowned upon, and essentially forbidden for officers, "since it would never work out."

I had been attending Episcopal services in the civilian community in Okinawa and was able to spend time with the missionary minister, Bill Heffner. He was a gifted speaker, writing and delivering his sermons in Japanese. He also tended the people at the leper colony, as well as holding services for the American military and civilian communities.

We asked him if he would marry us, but later found out that a colleague of his was the pastor in my hometown in Vermont, unlikely as that might seem. Informed by his colleague at my parents' request, he set up a long program of pre-marital Christian education for Sadako which would take nearly a year.

Next, we went to the Lutheran military chaplain who had agreed to marry us, but he was replaced by a Southern Baptist chaplain who just laughed at us.

There was a wonderful postscript to the Heffner episode. When we returned to work at the Adventist Hospital in 1963 as civilians, Rev. Heffner had left, and was replaced by a man named Browning, remarkably. We met when his son broke his ankle running around on a pool table.

Rev. Browning invited us for cocktails and related that Rev. Heffner had continued his "separate but equal" philosophy until his tour was almost over, at which time he discovered he was in love with his Okinawan parish secretary, married her, and took her to Texas for his next assignment!

In September there was "space available" on a military flight to Okinawa for the wedding. When my bride-to-be met me at the airport, she announced I had come at the wrong time, a bit of a set-back. In the old culture, apparently there were propitious days on the calendar, and not so favorable ones at other times. Then there was the necessary call to my parents from the Fighter Club the night before the wedding, which didn't go so well.

We met the Air Force Presbyterian chaplain, and he was willing to conduct the service at the beautiful Air Force Chapel on the Air Base, which was a far cry from the earlier plan of a wedding in a Navy Quonset hut.

We burned up precious leave time due to the necessity of getting married three times! Normally an Okinawan couple went to the city offices, where the bride's name would be transferred from her family's registry to that of the husband's and they were married! For us, the clerk had to scratch his head to figure out how to transfer my wife's name to that of a man with no "registry." The next day we reported to the Consulate for a civil marriage, necessary if the bride was to get a visa. On the fourth day we finally had the church wedding, which turned out very nicely despite all the politics. My squadron "friends" kept insisting that consummation of the marriage had to wait until after the "real" wedding.

A very happy day.

Bill Colohan, the mischief-maker who started all this was my best man. The Americans were in dress whites, and the bride wore a beautiful Western-style gown custom made for her. Her maid of honor was another pilot's wife.

The only man in her family who would give the bride away was an outcast of sorts. He attended college in the U.S. and for some reason had not done well with the family on return to Okinawa. He spoke fluent English and was a nice man.

There was a reception at the Fighter Club for family, friends, and squadron mates, The Navy officers and the enlisted men were all in dress whites, and the Okinawan ladies in kimonos. The enlisted men, always mischievous, plied the ladies with grasshoppers, a harmless looking green cocktail, laced with 2 different whiskies. After a couple of the green concoctions, one of the ladies giggled and asked Sadako, "How do you know which one is your husband? They all wear white uniforms and have big noses!"

We laughed at that, since one of the sailors had just asked me, "How do you know which one is your wife? They're all short, have black hair, and names that end in 'ko'."

Later in the afternoon there was an Okinawan reception at Mrs. Uehara's home, with another feast for a big crowd. One event does stands out in memory. Just as I was changing from dress whites into cooler casual dress, someone mistakenly opened the sliding door to the outside yard, and I was thus introduced to the whole village, standing on the platform in my boxer shorts!

At the time of our marriage, the squadron at Naha had been reclassified as a permanent duty assignment, making it easier to ship the legendary Buick convertible from Alameda to Okinawa, fixed up like new. We left in a blizzard of rice, driving north to Nago, a nice small country village, and stayed at a quiet country inn, or "yadoya." The doorman noted all the rice which had been showered on us as we left Naha and asked if he should pack it up for us.

We had reservations for the remainder of the week at a really nice officers' rest camp at Okuma on the northern end of the island. Our squadron was quite familiar with it, since there was a good dining room, and a short 1900-foot runway ending at the water's edge at both ends. We junior pilots had made it a practice to fly in for lunch frequently, and found it was possible to stop a Hellcat in 1900 feet. (Usually!)

The rest camp had a nice dining room, boats with drivers for water skiing, and idyllic scenery for just sitting. Ideal honeymoon, right? Not so fast!

We barely got settled before an enlisted man came around to our cottage with the news that we had to return to our duty station. The camp was closing due to an advancing typhoon. My protest that my duty station was in San Francisco was to no avail. We spent the rest of the visit at the Uehara home, giving the kids quarters to go see a movie, hoping to have a bit of privacy.

After returning to the U.S., the search for an apartment began. With concerns about prejudice or hostility, I was careful to tell each potential landlord that Sadako was Japanese. One lady took the news without comment and asked what I did for a living. When I responded that I was stationed at Moffett, she emphatically rejected me, saying "Nope, no Navy men!"

Sadako had to wait for Visa approval and a military transport ship to get to San Francisco, finally arriving just before Christmas 1958. George's wife Barbara was at the pier with me and brought a large bouquet of flowers for Sadako. I had met her when George was deployed on cruise and while we waited for them both to arrive, we occasionally dined together and compared notes. She was a lovely and talented person, the widow of his wingman who crashed into the ocean when a trim problem caused the airplane to dive into the ship's path directly on launch. I felt George was a fortunate man indeed.

FASRON 10

The duty station on return from Okinawa was a Fleet Support Squadron at Moffett Field, while awaiting discharge from the Navy to attend Stanford Medical School. The location of the base was fortunate since it provided a significant geographical advantage in applying for and getting interviews.

The people in the squadron were a good group and treated us well. The support activity included repair and testing of planes which were left behind when the squadrons deployed. Once again it was a great opportunity for one who loved to fly – I got to do test flights in the FJ-3 Fury, the F11-F Tiger, the F9F8 Cougar, the T-33 trainer, and the TF-1. The ancient Beechcraft was also a transport for local military events.

Getting off the transport plane from Okinawa at Travis AFB, I spied a '55 Chevy with a "for sale" sign in the window. It served us well during the entire five years of medical school. It did require a ring and valve job and a transmission change performed in the parking lot at student housing. For some reason, the rings from Sears locked up in the cylinders so the engine wouldn't even turn over. A fellow student towed the car to the top of the steepest hill in the area, and we let it coast downhill, but it only lurched to a halt in the middle of the road when the clutch was released. After redoing the job with a set of rings from a Chevy dealer, everything went perfectly.

On one of my flights, there was an "unsafe nose gear" warning while we were transporting a load of heavy parts, tools, and mechanics. The airplane had a "skag" or skid on the back end, and we figured if we could keep the nose gear off the ground, we might be able to avoid damaging the airplane. We moved any heavy cargo as far aft as possible and asked the largest mechanic to take his toolbox and sit on the toilet at the back end of the cabin during landing. We promised not to kid our mechanic and the plan worked! Although the airplane looked extremely odd with its nose way up in the air when we finished roll-out. We got a lineman to come out and put a lock pin in the errant gear, and the airplane suffered no damage.

Let Me Take It, Son

It seemed life was never dull in aviation. Our pilot training officer was the lead instructor in the TF-1 Tracker, a two pilot/nine passenger transport version of the Anti-Submarine Warfare (ASW) plane, the S2F. He had the most hours in that plane and often took the commanding officer to meetings or provided other utility services.

Another fine day, the training officer and another senior pilot were scheduled to take the boss and the other squadron C.O.s across the bay to NAS Alameda for a meeting.

Things began to unravel when the skipper and the C.O. of the jet training squadron decided they would like to fly the hop, although the C.O. of the jet training squadron had no experience in the plane, and the skipper had built up his flight hours mostly sleeping while I flew him to Long Beach to see his girlfriend. The plane commander gave them a quick briefing on takeoff and landing speeds and other basics.

The two qualified pilots were demoted to passenger status while the "big guys" started to take off. Before they passed the go-no-go point, the tower called, saying "You have an engine on fire!" For unknown reasons they continued but were not able to climb significantly in that configuration. Their acquaintance with procedures did not include things like single engine flight, shutting down and feathering the affected engine, raising the gear, keeping full power on the good engine, making sure the engine control friction locks were tight, and engaging a rudder boost. The deposed plane commander ran forward and managed to turn on the rudder boost, realized the situation was hopeless, and returned to his seat in the passenger compartment.

TF-1 Crash.

The aircraft missed the high-tension towers north of the field in San Francisco Bay but crashed upside down in shallow water. Miraculously, all escaped, and no one except the co-pilot was injured; he sustained a minor spine compression injury when he released his seat belt while still upside down.

During the accident investigation, the pilot said he did not retract the landing gear "for fear the tires would catch fire." The accident analysis revealed that the good engine was at idle, due to the loose control friction lock, the bad engine had not been feathered, and in that configuration with the gear down, it was impossible to maintain control. I was the squadron safety officer, and it was hard to put lipstick on that accident report!

"Vacation" at Nellis AFB

This was another episode of being chased by the devil, who seems to have had bad luck in corralling me although I was surely a good prospect.

As safety officer for the squadron, I had just read a report of vibration problems in the T-33, related to fatigued engine turbine blades breaking off and destroying the aircraft. To make matters worse, the turbine section of the engine was directly below the pilot's ejection seat. If the vibration did not immediately cease with power reduction, the recommended procedure was to shut down the engine and eject.

On a sunny Saturday afternoon, the squadron got a call from Nellis AFB in Las Vegas regarding a Navy jet trainer from Texas that had blown a tire on landing. The cynic might suspect that it was the pilot's effort to extend the weekend in Las Vegas rather than bad luck.

The Air Force didn't stock Navy tires and the nearest ones were at Moffett Field. For an enthusiastic pilot, this was yet another chance for flight time! The only aircraft available was our T-33, so the wheel and tire were loaded onto the back seat for the flight to Nevada on a beautiful afternoon.

After landing at Nellis and delivering the wheel to Maintenance, the search for the pilot was, as suspected, fruitless on a weekend in Vegas.

Navy regulations at that time called for the Command Duty Office to sign off the flight plan as clearing authority while the Maintenance Department confirmed the aircraft was ready for flight. A weather briefing was signed off by the meteorological officer.

At Nellis things seemed to be more relaxed. The Command Duty Officer was off base having supper. There was no maintenance officer around, and the only weather briefing available was by phone from a base in a different time zone.

No problem for the intrepid Naval Aviator! The Navy had two categories of instrument ratings for pilots. The first and most common was the "blue card" which allowed flights down to certain weather minimums and required command clearance for the flight. The coveted "green card" (not the one in the news these days) basically allowed more senior pilots to be their own clearance authority and to manage their own weather briefing.

Signing off as the maintenance authority, the weather authority, and the clearance authority was a bit dicey, since it meant I was responsible for everything associated with the flight, but that didn't look like a problem on a sunny afternoon in Vegas. The time spent trying to locate the lead-footed pilot and rousting out some troops to get fuel for the airplane delayed take-off until after sunset.

All checks and engine run-up passed muster. The tower gave clearance for take-off. Just as the nosewheel broke ground, the aircraft began to vibrate, and it increased rather than decreasing with power reduction while climbing out on take-off.

The vibration continued and at about 1000 to 1500 feet it seemed like the best of bad choices to shut down the engine. Ejection from the T-33 was not possible below 1000 feet, and not desirable below 2000 feet, usually ending badly if the chute does not fully deploy. In addition, the enlisted barracks were lined up just to the right of the runway.

Pilots who try to make a steep turn back to the take-off runway without power usually have that mentioned in their obituary. On the inbound flight I had noticed an old gravel covered runway, at a 60-degree angle from the main runway.

Informing the tower that I was shutting down and landing on the old runway, the tower operator asked for my position, and then saw the aircraft pretty much upside down as I was trying to regain control after losing hydraulic boost. He then offered the not very helpful information, "You can't land there! That runway's closed!" At that point the only possible response was "Roger. Gear down and locked." One's fantasy is always that the pilot sounds cool and collected, but suspect my voice was up an octave or two.

The landing in the dark was okay, but the runway was short, and covered with gravel. The end was fast approaching. The T-33 has two very heavy wingtip fuel tanks which can be jettisoned, and might have allowed stopping on the runway, but the red tank "jettison" button required two hands to access it, ever since a pilot inadvertently jettisoned tanks somewhere over Oakland. As I was shutting off electric power, the last communication I heard from the tower was something like, "You better not run off the end – there's a big ditch out there!" Thanks a lot.

The airplane did run off the end, and the big ditch really was there – one of those along the desert highways to handle the gully-washer rains sometimes seen in that area. Fortunately for the survival of a pilot with big troubles, the near wall of the ditch had a 30-45' incline upward, as did the opposite wall. The airplane, no longer in control, hit the incline, became briefly airborne, and hit the opposite wall, pretty much a pancake landing which broke the fuselage in half just behind the cockpit, and tore off both wings.

With the silliness which sets in after you find you're alive and unscathed, it seemed too bad to blow off the canopy and damage that too, but there was some urgency to departing, since the tires had been on fire for the last part of the roll-out.

Surveying the remains of my airplane and waiting for someone to join me, I smelled aviation gasoline, not jet fuel, which seemed odd. That never was explained, and since I had been dealing with other aspects prior to take-off, hadn't been able to supervise refueling.

Pretty soon, all the folks who had been home enjoying the weekend began arriving. The accident board was unable to pin down the cause of the vibration and surmised it might have been a faulty "shimmy damper" on the nosewheel, although that should have stopped immediately once the aircraft was off the ground and the gear retracted.

Meanwhile, back in California we had invited a tech rep my wife barely knew for dinner, and when I called to tell her I had crashed, she said, "You've got to come home – we're having company!" Everyone has their priorities.

Medical School

Moffett Field is quite close to Stanford University, which facilitated efforts to apply to medical school and have a live interview. The Navy obligation was finishing and after I was accepted there was an opportunity for a summer externship at the pediatric rehab facility near campus. During medical rounds the chief resident pointed out a teen-age girl who had a severe closed head injury after falling off a truck. She was unable to talk, couldn't move any limbs, and only blinked her eyes. Everyone thought she was a "vegetable" and he referred to her as such while passing by her bed.

As the group walked away, I saw her shed a tear, and there seemed to be more than vacancy in those eyes. I returned later and asked her to blink once for "yes," and twice for "no" to a couple of questions, and she made the appropriate responses immediately. Reaching way back to Navy training, it occurred to me that she might be able to learn to use Morse Code by blinking her eyes. She learned the entire alphabet in less than one week! It was really exciting to find that it was all still there inside but couldn't get out.

Some good folks at Hewlett Packard were open to the idea of constructing something which might translate the blinking into audible Morse Code letters, and they built a primitive transistor gadget to attach to eyeglass frames. We put heavy black eye shadow on her eyelid, and had her blink to activate a little buzzer, "long" for dashes and "short" for dots. The white of her eye was the "off" and the darkened eyelid was the "on." The dot and dash sounds depended on the pattern of blinks. She amazed us with her quick acquisition of skills with the device, and the nurses worked hard to learn to translate the code to English. Much later we found we had overlooked the fact that she could move one finger as well, and she was able to transition to tapping on an HP electric typewriter, which was quite new at the time.

In 1964, Stanford Med made major changes in the curriculum, extending the program from four to five years (along with the extra year's tuition, of course.) The plan was highly innovative, with three pre-clinical years instead of the usual two. The planners thought that students might be allowed to start during their fourth year of college, gaining their bachelor's degree at the end of the first medical school year. It turned out that the vast majority of the applicants were those with advanced degrees, a civilian career, or military background, and were a much older age group than those in most medical programs.

Another major change was a schedule of large blocks of free time in the program, which might be used to pursue research, volunteer work, or even "open" time for reading or other individual activities.

The pre-clinical courses in biochemistry were taught by a faculty including Drs. Berg, Kornberg, and Lederberg, three Nobel Prize winners at the dawn of DNA research. Anatomy, Physiology, and Pharmacology spanned three years, with the professorial option of including material from any year on any exam. Fortunately for some of us, exams were graded on a pass-fail basis rather than a letter grade.

I was able to snag a job as a helper in the Pharmacology department under an enthusiastic professor working on the mystery of transfer of information from DNA to RNA.

John Daniels was my lab partner and good friend, and we were assigned to advanced research involving DNA-RNA transfer with two groups of chickens, some who received large doses of estrogen and some who did not. After each experiment was finished, we took home the bunch of chickens to supplement our food supply. Plucking the chickens in the student housing area was not wildly popular! Some students also had qualms about eating the chickens which had been given large doses of estrogen, but none of us were affected. John went on to a productive academic career, as well as racing airplanes!

In Okinawa, the squadron owned a really ugly 1946 Fraser stick shift automobile. With help, my wife had learned to drive in that car on the Yonabaru airstrip, which did offer some favorable aspects for the novice driver, since there was nothing to crash into and no concerns with center lines and red lights.

Bunny Browning was literally buried by the stack of baby gifts she received at a shower prior to her departure on maternity leave. Shown with her are Martha Parrish, left, and Jen Eile, friends in Special Products. Her baby, born June 11, is a girl named Elizabeth.

Sadako/Bunny at Fairchild.

She later put the skill to good use during medical school. To supplement my meager income as a medical student, she first got a job in a Japanese restaurant which was frequented by executives from Fairchild Semiconductor. They had developed a preference for Japanese women on the transistor fabrication, since they showed more concentration and better dexterity with the microscopes. They hired Sadako (who they nicknamed Bunny) and a number of the waitresses to work on the transistor assembly line.

The electronics industry was in its infancy at the time and each transistor was fabricated individually, and then connected to the circuit board. Sadako eventually got assigned to work on experimental products, fabricating multiple transistors under one "hat," as the covers were called. We've come a long way since then!

My plans were to wait until after medical school for children. Apparently Sadako had other ideas, and I was surprised and delighted with the arrival of Suzie in 1962.

The Mark Hopkins Hotel

Someone at medical school introduced me to a guy who got me to share a window washing job at the Top of the Mark, a cocktail lounge on the 19th floor of the Mark Hopkins Hotel in San Francisco. The pay was very good and the work dangerous enough that the unions didn't want to touch it. After a short orientation to the technique of washing the windows inside and outside by my partner, I was left on my own.

Mark Hopkins Hotel.

The windows were originally constructed so they could be rotated around a horizontal axis and washed from inside. The building inspectors worried about patrons falling out of the windows and ordered they be welded shut. That posed a problem since the main attraction to get patrons in for expensive drinks was the grand view of the city through spotless windows.

Every Sunday the windows had to be washed inside and out. The worker playing spider on the outside wall wore a belt, attached by ropes and pulleys to eye bolts on the five corners of the building.

To hook those up, it was necessary to crawl out an elevator access window, climb up one story from the bar, attach the ropes to the eye bolts, then lower oneself down one floor on the outside to the window ledges, lugging a bucket and squeegee.

There was no safety rope while hooking the pulleys to the corners of the building, and with a bit of dew or wind, it could be thrilling. Once the ropes were hooked up, they were adjusted while the window cleaner worked progressively across the building. The excess rope, after being lashed to the belt just hung down and swung in the wind. The worst was when there had been fog, and the ledges were wet; the best was when it rained, and you got paid for not working.

I rigged a safety rope tied corner to corner and connected it to the belt in case of a fall. That was soon removed by the senior partner who said it "slowed him down."

The pulley arrangement provided a 4:1 advantage allowing one to climb back up one floor to the access window with a 40- to 50-pound pull; but if the rope came loose from the belt, one couldn't manage the 4:1 disadvantage, nearly 800 pounds. And if the rope got disconnected, it was a 19-story fall to the street.

It took most of the morning to clean all the windows. Usually the inside was done first, since the old ladies came in early from the Cathedral across the street for their Sunday martinis. They were intrigued by a person standing just outside the window, 19 stories up. One day the rope got disconnected from the belt, leaving me hanging in space, with that 4:1 disadvantage and unable to hang on except by clamping the rope in my teeth and then slowly swinging the rope around my leg enough times that it could be coaxed back into place. Instead of calling for help, the assembled crowd just pointed and laughed!

Another day, the bucket of water got unhooked, and fell 19 floors to the ground at the front entrance. I rushed down to see if I had killed anybody. The uniformed doorman didn't get hit, said nothing, and just pointed to the bucket he had kicked into the bushes. He was a stoic individual. After a few months, sitting exhausted on the roof, pondering my likely fate, looking across the Bay to the Naval Air Station at Alameda, it occurred to me, "They're wearing parachutes and they're closer to the ground than I am!" That same day I signed up for the Naval Air Reserves, and since then have only washed windows on the ground floor.

Medical Aviator

During that time in medical school there were two S2F ASW squadrons at Alameda for reserve officer training. The "weekend warriors" had two or three days of training and flying once a month, usually starting with a night flight on Friday and other requirements during the weekend. The airplanes were quite familiar from our previous active-duty days, and the break from school was welcome. If the weather was bad, the weekend began with happy hour.

S2F Tracker.

There was one pilot who always flew in the right (co-pilot) seat with me, and he had a fascinating habit. Part of routine training was practicing stalls. Every time I pulled the nose up until the airplane began to shudder, he would begin to rhythmically slap his hand on his knee and then slap his oxygen mask. It seemed to be entirely automatic with him and could be repeated at any time. He remained a co-pilot for the duration.

One weekend two of us planned a flight to NAS Whidbey Island near Seattle with a return Saturday morning. The weather forecast was benign, and we had plenty of fuel for the 700-mile trip, with a calculated endurance of 1100 miles.

We took off just after dark, in good weather, which unfortunately didn't last. As we approached the Oregon border we began to pick up icing at 10,000 feet. The S2F had excellent alcohol prop deicing, and inflatable "boots" on the wings and tail, but the ice was building up behind the boots and the ice chips flying off the propellor blades beating a tattoo on the fuselage exactly at head level was disconcerting.

At military (full) power we were able to maintain altitude, but only at minimum airspeed. We called Center to request a lower altitude, hoping to get below freezing level, and got this cheery response, "You can have any altitude you want – you're the only one up there. Just remember the mountains are at 7000 feet."

At this rate of fuel burn, Seattle was out of the question, and with lots of moving elbows, pencils, and flashlights, we planned a destination change to Portland, which had a National Guard facility.

It was raining in Portland when we landed, with some ice still clinging to parts of the plane. The National Guard folks treated us well and after a good night's sleep, breakfast, and clear skies, going home was a welcome relief.

The opportunity to fly continued until the Berlin Crisis in 1961, when President Kennedy ordered up a number of Reserve and National Guard units to active duty in response to the Soviet closure of access to Berlin and erection of the Berlin Wall. One of our two reserve squadrons was called up. Our squadron was spared for the moment, but it was a shock to consider the prospect of dropping out of medical school for an indeterminate period.

Apparently, that issue also had some significance nationally, since many small towns began to lose their only physician or surgeon to active duty. This led to the decision by President Kennedy to exclude physicians or medical students from any reserve units other than the Medical Corps. This was tough, but not an everlasting banishment from the sky.

Okinawa Part Two

Choosing to have the two blocks of Stanford's "open" time placed adjacent to the summer break between the fourth and fifth years at Stanford made it possible to get more than six months of elective "free" time.

We learned of an opportunity to work at the Adventist Medical Center in Okinawa, and I fear I neglected medical courses while taking two years of spoken and written Japanese at Stanford, under a professor who was a descendant of the man on the 100,000 yen note. He was a great teacher and a hard taskmaster. Our reading assignment during the second semester was to read an entire Nobel Prize winning novel in Japanese. Our tests and written reports were also in Japanese.

For most medical students the cost of transportation for a family of three to Japan would be prohibitive; however, a classmate who had been a Marine Major was able to get free passage overseas for his block time with the Peace Corps on a ship owned by the Marcona Mining company, based in the Bay area.

He suggested contacting the company, and we went for an interview. The company bent the rules a bit, since a physician was required if a small child was on board. They decided I was "sort of" a doctor, and kindly allowed us passage from San Francisco to Kobe, Japan, on the San Juan Traveler, a dual-purpose ship nearly the size of an aircraft carrier with a cargo capacity of 50,000 tons of iron ore, or a similar amount of crude oil.

The route was not quite direct, since the ship sailed to Peru to load iron ore, then crossed the Pacific to Kobe, Japan, unloaded the ore, sailed to Indonesia, cleaned the cargo hold enroute, and loaded crude oil which was carried back to San Francisco.

We were berthed in the Owner's Suite of rooms with a splendid view of everything. We brought suitcases for a 6-month stay, a playpen, and medical books for study during the 35-day trip to Japan.

Sadako and Suzie at sea.

The captain was an American, and the Chief Engineer a Canadian, both gracious hosts who invited us to join them for meals. There were three or four Japanese officers who sometimes ate in the captain's dining room, and sometimes ate with the rest of the Japanese crew.

My wife and I and our one-year-old baby girl sailed under the Golden Gate Bridge, beginning a true adventure during the summer of 1963. Departing from San Francisco, we sailed south to the west coast of Peru. The small coastal town was completely owned by the Marcona Company, which supplied housing, food, clothing, and all necessities. Water for drinking, plumbing, and irrigation had to be shipped in by tanker since it was said that the area had not had rain in 100 years.

It required 36 hours to load the 50,000 tons of ore, directly from the mines in the hills to the hold of the ship on a very long conveyor belt, accompanied by a thick coat of dust enveloping everything.

The town also had a hospital run by an American doctor and our captain arranged an afternoon escape from the dust to visit the hospital. The doctor was cordial, erudite, and a good host, even offering a glass of Johnny Walker Scotch which was not available on board. He told us he had a daughter at Stanford. I don't recall if she was a pre-med or not.

Even though it was winter in the Southern Hemisphere, it was warm outside, and we were happy to leave the dust behind. Crossing the Pacific was a pleasant interlude, with study, entertaining a one-year-old, and keeping the toddler from falling overboard.

The thoughtful Japanese cooks made a birthday cake for her first birthday, and sometimes served a Japanese dinner to the delight of my Okinawan wife. The Japanese language study paid off in more interaction with the officers and crew.

Medical emergencies could be a problem since commercial ships were limited to getting advice by radio from island stations that had doctors assigned. The distance from shore usually eliminated the possibility of extracting an ill or injured crewman by helicopter.

On one occasion a sailor from our ship developed a painful abscess and a high fever. There was no medical facility on board, scant medical supplies, and no modern antibiotics. Since evacuation was not possible, the island consultants advised hot compresses as the only option.

It seemed to me that this man was too sick to tolerate a prolonged infection, and the possibility of opening the abscess was discussed with the captain. He felt we weren't authorized to do this but didn't get upset when I went ahead and did the minor surgery anyway without anesthesia. The patient's immediate response was gratifying to an "almost doctor," and he promptly became afebrile and returned to duty.

Just as we were becoming used to the luxury of being the only guests on board, we arrived in the harbor at Kobe, where the iron ore was unloaded by huge clamshell cranes at the Sumitomo Iron Works.

Reluctantly leaving ship, we faced the challenge of getting transportation for the 1000-mile trip to Okinawa and ended up on a rickety steamer with no air conditioning, sleeping on the floor with 40 other passengers. There were nasty young men reaching through the fully open windows from the outside passageways to grope the women. I don't remember whether we had food, but we were very happy to be off the ship and met by my wife's family and the staff from the Adventist Medical Center in Naha.

We were to live at Sadako's mother's home in a suburb called Oroku. The hospital was located across the city, perhaps ten miles away. The bus was usually filled with school students. I was at least a head taller than anyone else, trying to stay upright as the bus navigated the winding roads, while our young one was toddling around with her mother or grandmother and mingling with the many kids in the neighborhood.

There was a small general store near home which had the only telephone in town. Once the men learned I spoke Japanese, they were very cordial, and the owner even came to the house to wake me during the night if there was an emergency at the hospital.

The Adventist Hospital had an ambulance of questionable reliability. It was a nice contribution from one of the American auto dealers, but it nearly came to a bad end when someone tried to drive to a nearby island connected by a sand bar at low tide and the ambulance got marooned midway. It was said that only the rotating red light on the roof was visible when rescue attempts were made. It was repaired, but the electrical functions were sporadic from then on.

We often needed to visit the Army Hospital, where we got military mail service, in exchange for reading all their tuberculosis screening chest x-rays for them. On one of those runs, I decided to fight the traffic using the red light and siren to get back to our hospital. Unfortunately, the errant vehicle chose that moment to break down on the highway, leaving me with the embarrassing task of explaining to helpful motorists why there were no patients on board!

The nurses at the hospital were kind, dedicated, and well-trained. Even though the Adventist diet was vegetarian, and coffee was taboo, they would sneak cups of Sanka to me on duty nights. There were two physicians, including an older Okinawan doctor who had been trained before the war. His ability to speak both Japanese and Okinawan was a valuable asset.

Many of the patients suffered from skin conditions with eczema caused by scratching in the heat and high humidity. I was told that the old ladies thought their skin condition was due to syphilis, although they were celibate widows ever since the end of the war. The Okinawan doctor was able to restore them with shots of B-12, which apparently gave quite a jolt!

Dr. Meinhardt, the director, was a saint by any reckoning. He was a wonderful, dedicated physician and a great mentor. It was a real privilege to work with him.

Most days there were over 200 outpatient visits. With such a busy schedule, he still enforced a 15- to 30-minute supine rest before the afternoon clinic which was quite restorative.

Most of the clinic visits were for skin problems or trauma, and most of the in-patient care was for obstetrics. The two years of Japanese at Stanford proved critical while working in the clinic. Some of the older patients spoke only Okinawan, but the nurses were always ready to assist with translation from Okinawan to Japanese. The senior nurse was another saint; a leader, translator, and midwife as well.

We saw a wide range of serious medical problems and trauma. I made my first diagnosis of a new case of leprosy.

Dr. Meinhart and I alternated duty every other night, almost all of which was obstetrical care and deliveries. After brief tutelage Dr. Meinhart put me on my own, but he was available as back-up since he lived in a home on the hospital grounds. I don't remember ever having to call him, though, since the senior nurse/midwife always assisted, translated, and got me out of trouble on some occasions.

Deliveries were all vaginal, with only one Caesarian section in six months, a story for later. Twins were common, as were breech presentations. One night there was an unusual case of a normal birth, followed by an atrophied miniature which looked like a "gumby" attached to the placenta. There were no catastrophes with the many breech births delivered feet first, leading me to wonder why so many in the U.S. turned into surgical deliveries.

We had a pregnant lady arrive in labor with untreated miliary tuberculosis throughout her lungs, and another in labor in an untreated diabetic coma. Managing the delivery wasn't a problem, but the babies had a tough time and may not have survived since complex neonatal care was a thing of the future.

My midwife assistant always seemed to be there when most needed and once saved me by taking over delivery of a placenta accreta, where the placenta does not separate from the uterus, which if handled incorrectly can lead to uterine rupture and death.

Midway through the year there was a squabble dividing the church, which sounded a bit silly to an outsider; something called the Brinsmead Doctrine, regarding whether those living on earth at the Last Day would know they were saved before they died, or after. Dr. Meinhardt apparently was on the wrong side of the argument and was forced to resign and leave the island. When he and his family left, they gave all their possessions, including their automobile and home to the hospital. It was a terrible loss.

He was replaced by a younger doctor from the Tokyo Adventist Hospital, an American who had completed one year of residency in surgery and did not speak Japanese. We worked together for several months, during which time a pregnant patient was admitted at term and on exam I thought she had a placenta previa, a condition in which the placenta blocks the opening from the uterus, preventing vaginal delivery.

The surgeon's diagnosis was a breech presentation, and he wanted the patient to continue in labor. Only when she began to bleed heavily, and her blood count sank dangerously did he come around to agree with the medical student's diagnosis.

In this situation, a procedure called a Caesarian Section (C-section) must be used to extract the baby through a large incision in the abdomen to save the mother and child. The doctor from Tokyo had assisted at one such surgery, while I had never even seen one. Left with no alternatives, however, we took her to the O.R. on an emergency basis. The incision in the abdomen for the C-section was not well placed, and the operative field sprouted a whole bouquet of vessel clamps as we tried to staunch the bleeding.

The male nurse anesthetist was not helping to calm us, as he progressively reported her status in Japanese. "Blood pressure 60, blood pressure 30." Then "blood pressure unobtainable." The wound suction went to an open stainless container which could hold several liters. The rising level was alarming. The hospital did not have a blood bank, so the only option was to give more saline fluid and pray. There was profound relief all around when we delivered a live baby, got the wound sutured, and noted a weak pulse return.

The Army Medical Center had an agreement with us to provide blood, but only a physician could pick it up, and it was a 15-to 20-mile drive with white knuckles to the hospital in horrible traffic. We obtained several units of blood, and this time our ambulance didn't fail.

Both the lady and the baby survived and did well after the transfusion. The notes said that the woman's hematocrit was 20 percent when we went to the O.R., and less than 8 percent at the end of surgery. (Normal is above 40 percent). I spoke with the patient in recovery and asked how she felt. Her remarkable response was, "All right, but I'm a little light-headed when I sit up."

Our time with these good people ended before Christmas, and the hospital graciously contributed the airfare to Chicago where our family gathered for the holidays with our toddler and her cousins wildly enjoying the luxury of a western home. We returned to Palo Alto for the remainder of the senior year, before heading east for the one-year internship in Grand Rapids, Michigan.

Internship

After finishing the fifth and final year of the program at Stanford Medical School, we all scrambled to find good internships for the next year. One which got a lot of favorable reviews was at Blodgett Memorial Hospital in Grand Rapids, Michigan, which had a good reputation for location and teaching, as well as free housing on campus.

One of our more unfortunate choices was giving up the '55 Chevy which had served us well through five years of medical school. We bought a Nash Rambler Wagon since we felt we needed a larger vehicle to take all our belongings to Michigan and with the prospect of another child on the way.

It was a huge mistake to buy the car from a "kindly" dealer in Redwood City who convinced us it was a bargain (after he had put sawdust in the transmission to quiet it down). We took the southern route to avoid the highest mountains and rented a U-Haul trailer for books and furniture.

After watching the radiator boil for 400 miles, we stopped in Barstow, mailed 1500 pounds of books to our destination, and followed a watering truck up the Rockies for some desperately needed auxiliary cooling.

All the intern families lived in an apartment building on the hospital campus and many friendships developed. We all had to wear white uniforms with large name plates, which had the look of a pharmacist's coat.

The chief resident, who was a bit to the right politically, took our new group of interns on a tour of the wards and addressed an old lady lying in bed, unresponsive to his greeting or mental status questions. Finally, he said, "Who is the President?" To which she immediately bolted upright, and said in a loud voice, "Johnson's my president!" Following which he pronounced, "There's a Democrat for you!"

He did have many redeeming qualities. One weekend he invited me to go to the woods to hunt for mushrooms. He knew the edible ones well and the poisonous ones from study. We collected a nice basket full and took them back to housing. All the wives were sure we were eating toadstools and would die shortly. They watched wide eyed, expecting us to keel over before we finished a bowl of nicely cooked mushrooms.

Suzie and me ready for dinner.

My wife Sadako even made a tiny nurse's uniform for our daughter to wear to Sunday dinner at the hospital.

The Rambler wagon continued to be a problem. As my grandmother used to say, "You can't make a silk purse out of a sow's ear." I tried to do a ring and valve job at Christmastime. It was a chilly task in the Michigan parking lot in December but got easier after the maintenance crew took pity and let me use their heated garage at the hospital.

The nurses were very helpful and kind. Almost all the nurses were graduates of a local nursing school, and a few were a bit "provincial."

Our son Will was born during that year during my rotation in the ER. I couldn't be there during the delivery but hurried to the nursery at 2:00 or 3:00am. When I asked the elderly nurse to see the Browning baby, her response was "Oh, we put him back in the corner – he's a Mongoloid, you know!"

I had not considered the prospect of returning to the Navy after I was rejected for a military scholarship program which offered financial help during senior year at Stanford.

The chief of Surgery at Blodgett was Dr. J.D. Miller, who was also an admiral in the Medical Corps Reserve. He suggested I consider the Scientist Astronaut program which was ramping up at that time.

After hearing my tale of rejection, he did some research on my behalf and found that the Navy's Bureau of Personnel and the Bureau of Medicine did not share any fitness reports, security clearances, or other required documents. In spite of the enlistment office's assurance to the contrary, my application was discarded as "incomplete," rather than "rejected."

With the help of Dr. Miller, my application to the program at the School of Aviation Medicine in Pensacola was approved. The prospect of returning to flying was welcome.

Our growing family packed up our brand-new Plymouth station wagon in June and headed from Michigan to Pensacola, leaving the Rambler to a well-deserved fate.

The academic program at the AvMed School was quite worthwhile, with lectures in aviation medicine, ENT (ear, nose, and throat) problems, psychology, and cardiology. There was training outside the classroom, including ejection seat training, survival school at Eglin AFB, and low-pressure chamber training which simulated trying to survive removing oxygen masks at 18,000 feet, then 36,000 feet (with careful supervision and rapid return of oxygen supply by the techs).

Ejection seat training.

An ejection seat ride was required, as well as a mandatory one-mile swim, and training in the "Dilbert Dunker," a fiendish device containing a pilot's seat and harness, on a 45-degree incline which dumped the student into the water at a good rate of speed, then tipped upside down, leaving him to extricate himself, while divers stood by.

Some of my classmates didn't take the academic program very seriously, probably thinking of it as a "paid vacation" after the arduous past five years.

The class valedictorian got the choice of any Naval Air Station in the world, which was a great stimulus for me to work for it. My wife was urging return to Okinawa but assignment to a patrol plane squadron there didn't sound that exciting. Some blessed person urged me to consider VX-4, the air development and test squadron at Point Mugu, California, a suggestion for which I remain eternally grateful.

PENSACOLA

Return to Flying

I was able to join the highly sought-after program for pilots who had been Naval Aviators, then went to medical school, then returned to flying after completing the course at the School of Aerospace Medicine. Those fliers with dual designations were able to perform the duties of a flight surgeon and an aviator. At that time, there were only twelve so designated.

When the academic course was finished, our next stop was the Naval Air Station in Meridian, Mississippi, for refresher flight training. The advanced training program included formation flying, navigation, night flying, and carrier qualification.

The civilians in Meridian were gracious despite our mixed marriage, and we made good friends while there. The flying was in the T2A, and my first instructor, John Westerman was relieved not to have a "newbie" for the first formation flight. That flight tends to be harrowing for instructors since the student can make all kinds of mistakes resulting in a midair collision.

T2A jet trainer.

Our families, both with little kids, became good friends, and we spent pleasant nights with them playing bridge while the kids slept wherever they chose.

Already a lieutenant and an aviator, I was included in the instructors' happy hours, which was interesting indeed. John McCain was among the instructors, and he had cut a wide swath. He was single at the time, a hell raiser, and the self-proclaimed "Commodore" of the Meridian Yacht Club (of which he was the sole member, with a raft in a pond on base as his flagship).

That assignment was followed by a return to Pensacola for jet carrier qualifications on the USS Lexington. My mother and dad were visiting us and happened to arrive when guests were being invited on board to view flight operations. Landing on the angled deck was a new experience.

On the old straight deck carriers, once you got the "cut" from the Landing Signal Officer (LSO), you were committed to land and hoped you snagged a wire before crashing into the "barrier" that protected the planes on the forward deck. On the angled deck, as you touched down, full power was added in case of a "hook skip" over all four arresting gear cables. In that event the airplane was safely airborne again for another try.

There also was a more modern variant of the "mirror" called the Fresnel Lens, which had a row of lights to indicate whether the plane was high, low, or on the "ball" (the correct line-up). The LSO augmented that with voice commands, speed control, and approach instructions.

That day our flight of five included an instructor, two Navy pilots, a Marine, and a NavCad. One turned back toward shore when he announced that he had lost radio contact, although we could hear him, and he responded to orders from the instructor. (I guess he just wasn't in the mood for carrier-type excitement that day.) The other Navy student pilot got his five landings or "traps" and left for home with the instructor. Next was the Marine cadet, who overshot the turn and came back, crossed the landing line, and ended up catching the number four wire, and crashed into the Fresnel Lens on the edge of the flight deck.

We had to orbit the ship until deck crew got the pilot out of the cockpit and lifted the precariously tilted airplane free and out of the way so we could complete our five required landings.

By the time we had a "ready deck" and the required five traps were completed, I didn't have enough fuel to get back to Pensacola, so it was necessary to remain in the pattern and land on the carrier for refueling. I was delighted with the prospect of the extra landing, but the "Air Boss" not so much. While I was at the fueling station near the island of the carrier, he dropped a few unkind words on me for upsetting the rhythm of his day.

To make things worse, the civilian guests aboard were invited to lunch in the officers' dining room. My mother, sitting next to the Air Boss, was rhapsodical about my performance including the extra landing. That undoubtedly required superhuman virtue for him not to say what he thought about the matter.

F9F-9 Cougar

Next stop for the overstuffed station wagon was Kingsville, Texas, near Corpus Christi. Kingsville was a lovely breezy city on the Gulf for introduction to our first combat airplane, the F9F Cougar, a swept wing fighter. Familiarization flights were followed by formation and gunnery against a banner towed by another F9. It was great fun, a feeling perhaps not shared so much by the pilot towing the banner, hoping we would aim at the correct target. After that last requirement was met, we packed up again, and struck out for our "real" duty station at Point Mugu, California, along the southern route.

The station wagon was now fitted out with after-market air conditioning which had to be shut off after the radiator over-heated. At 105 degrees, tempers were a bit frayed. In those days, without seat belts, our son loved to jump up and down in the back seat which tended to upset undigested food. After progressive stern warnings to sit down, he finally barfed the whole breakfast down the back of my neck. Screeching to a halt, I grabbed him by the straps on his little overalls and held him over the edge of the bridge over an arroyo while he continued to lose the rest of his breakfast. His sister apparently thought I was going to toss him and bedlam ensued. He did sit quietly for a little while after that.

We found an inviting motel with a large pool and decided to stop there. They were shut down because their A/C was out of service but did let us enjoy the pool before continuing.

Sadako's last pregnancy stretched from Pensacola to Meridian to Pensacola to Texas to Point Mugu, where our youngest son, Michael, was born very shortly after we arrived. He was a happy baby.

We got into senior base housing the day we arrived, but after the delivery, we were moved to "more appropriate" quarters for a lieutenant's family. We and the children were quite happy with the arrangements.

Son Michael was very young and reminded us of Swee'Pea (from the Popeye cartoons). He had a habit of sneaking off to the neighbor's house. Said neighbor had a mischievous sense of humor and when he appeared to investigate the closet, she closed the door. When Sadako came over frantically looking for him, the door was opened to find him fast asleep.

We did get a call from base security when son Will (age 3 or 4) and another friend decided to visit their dads' squadrons on the other side of the base, mounted their tricycles, and started down the base main highway during the 8 o'clock rush hour. They were returned unharmed!

VX-4 was the only fighter squadron on the base. The officers were nearly all experienced pilots or flight officers, and the wives were a congenial, easy-going bunch. The flying was ideal with both F-4 Phantoms and F-8 Crusaders, a T-33, and an old Beechcraft SNB, a two-engine tail wheel small transport which was quite quirky on landing. I enjoyed all of them.

Nello Pierozzi

Shortly after I arrived, Nello Pierozzi, became the skipper for most of the time I was there from '66 to '69. Nello had been a member of the Blue Angels way back and still was in touch with many old comrades, and he was one of the most colorful people I have ever met.

When Nello first joined the squadron, I was assigned to give him an area familiarization flight. The squadron had a T-33, a two-seat straight wing trainer from the '50s used as a utility aircraft. He was in the front seat and immediately after take-off headed out to sea and found a carrier to which he had been assigned in the past.

He began to make carrier landing approaches, although the T-33 doesn't have a hook and couldn't land on a carrier. The C.O. apparently was a buddy of his, and played along, turning the ship away each time Nello got lined up on final!

With his past in the Blues, Nello was quite aware of the importance of good public relations. Each year we would take a squadron portrait, with all pilots and NFOs (Naval Flight Officers) in clean flight suits and an F-4 and an F-8 behind us and with Nello in front. Most of the pilots were 6 feet or better but Nello made the most of his 5 feet 8 inches. As the photographer was about to take the portrait, Nello would turn to us and order us to bend our knees to minimize the height discrepancy; as soon as he turned back to face the photographer, we would all stand on tiptoe!

VX-4 Squadron photo.

Medical Duties

A project which came up soon was generated by a finding on the C.O.'s annual x-ray. The film showed some shadows called "coin lesions" looking a bit like silver dollars in both lungs. These are seen in tuberculosis and were quite worrisome in a healthy asymptomatic pilot. His vital lung capacity was markedly decreased from the normal 5 liters to 3 liters. On a repeat x-ray the next day, they had disappeared!

The squadron had a portable compact spirometer, which measures lung volume, and I was able to get pulmonary capacity data from all the pilots in the cockpit immediately before flight and immediately after landing after air combat maneuvering flights. The same result was found in many of the pilots. The worst results were in smokers. Their lung volume would be down by 40 percent after a 45-minute simulated air-to-air combat exercise.

Research revealed that at high G forces, all the blood in the lungs goes to the area below the heart, while oxygenation remains uniform throughout. With each breath the oxygen is completely absorbed from the air sacs below the level of the heart, causing them to collapse and appear dense on x-ray. Once on the ground the oxygen and blood distribution become balanced again and the lesions disappear by the next day.

The study was accepted for publication in the Aerospace Medical Journal. It turns out that the U.S was tripped up by technology. Our aircraft had a 5-liter bottle of liquid oxygen, which provided 100 percent oxygen to the lungs. Our Iron Curtain colleagues were behind in technology, and used a system we had abandoned, called diluter demand. Their oxygen was stored in pressurized tanks, and the breathing systems mixed oxygen from the tank with ambient air, which is 20 percent oxygen and 80 percent nitrogen. The nitrogen in the inhaled air prevented the air sacs from collapsing, so the problem did not exist in their aircraft.

The folks at the Bureau felt that the problem was not significant enough to warrant changing the existing systems, although I had concerns about the loss of endurance if a pilot had to eject and escape in combat.

Dispensary Duties

Due to the involvement in both flying and medicine, relationships with the dispensary were peculiar — most of the time was spent on the flight line, and the medical duties were mostly primary care for the squadron personnel and their wives and kids. There was also frequent on-call duty for after-hours emergencies.

Except for cases of smog-generated bronchitis, people usually weren't very sick at Mugu, so I had time for a review of the local epidemic of hangovers. With the help of the pharmacy, we did a double-blind study of various over-the-counter medicines, along with Alka Seltzer. There were no significant improvements, however.

There were some medical emergencies on base. One helicopter pilot who fit into the "Shoulda been dead" crowd had an engine failure and a crash landing in the commissary parking lot. Fortunately, there were no injuries. Later he and his son were riding on his motorcycle when he crashed into a century plant, with its sword-like spikes, which impaled his cheek and almost did a tonsillectomy on the other side of his throat. With concern for the magnitude of the injury and possible involvement of his throat, I told him we would refer him immediately to a specialist at the Naval Hospital at Long Beach or San Diego. The referral was met with firm rejection from the plastic surgery and ENT departments at both hospitals. It was a bit awkward to inform him that I had found a specialist and it was me.

The cheek injury repair was successful, and the oral wounds healed but he was left with a fashionable scar. There was no love lost for unavailable hospital based "specialists."

One routine visit at the dispensary led to facing a great deal of kidding. Most of the squadron wives saw me for their annual checkup and the "mandatory" pelvic exam. One of the wives, a hairdresser from Texas, tended to be colorful and always entertaining. She came in for her annual physical and after the usual pleasantries, was on the exam table with her legs in the stirrups, appropriately draped with a sheet.

The equipment in our facility left something to be desired. I failed to notice that one wheel was missing from the rolling stool at the foot of the table was, and as I sat down, it tipped over, dumping me to the floor with a loud crash. She pushed down the sheet, peered down at me, then asked whether I had never seen anything like that or whether she had some horrible disease!

Squadron Projects

As an Air Development Squadron, we were assigned a variety of missions including testing new countermeasure against the SAM missiles, developing improvements in air combat maneuvering against each other, or against some Soviet MiGs, which somehow had arrived at a site in the desert near Nellis AFB.

VX-4 Attacks Lake Havasu with Lance the Adventurer

Soon after checking in to the squadron, several of us "newbies" were assigned to an "area reconnaissance flight" with a more senior pilot for familiarization with the southern California terrain, in case of radio or navigation failure.

Two of us were flying F-8 Crusaders and "Lance" was flying an F-4 Phantom. Lance was adventurous to a fault, an excellent chef, a reputed wine connoisseur, a roué, and a pretty good pilot, although daring to the extreme.

He chose to take us to Lake Havasu on the Arizona border where his friends were expecting us. The first low pass in formation at 100 to 200 feet was excellent. Then Lance told us to "dirty up" (gear down, flaps down) for a slow speed pass while he made a high-speed pass just above us. After that run, he made a high rolling climb and said he would join us on departure.

He misjudged his dive a bit, and all we could see was a Phantom descending rapidly in a high nose-up attitude, both burners going, and we were sure he was going in the water. After making a rooster tail in the lake at nearly ground level and blowing over a tent his friends had pitched on a sand spit, we made a hasty departure.

Some folks at Havasu didn't take to our little air show and demanded our friends report the violation by the aircraft. Since Lance's friends were dastardly Navy sympathizers, they insisted the airplanes were Air Force planes from Las Vegas. I guess those poor guys got lined up for a "confession inspection."

After returning to base, our flight leader and his wife invited us to dinner at their home on base. Lance, the wine connoisseur, opened an expensive bottle of wine, tasted it, made a bad face, and poured it down the drain. We were certainly not wealthy at that point in our careers, so I was impressed.

In addition to being a good host and raconteur, he was quite unconventional. There was a belief among some pilots that the marriage license becomes invalid outside a radius of 200 miles, and Lance certainly put that theory to the test.

On one occasion he asked the skipper to authorize him to fly to D.C. about a secret project, but the story goes that he only made it to Cannon Air Force Base in New Mexico. There he met a lady friend, rented a car, drove to a resort at Taos, and checked in.

After a relaxing afternoon, they went to dinner. Lo and behold, our intrepid adventurer spotted the only other couple in the dining room and realized that they were also from Point Mugu. With more Chutzpah than good sense, he steered his "friend" directly to their table and asked to join them. Apparently, the surprised couple was more traditional, and departed without finishing their meal!

On another occasion, the squadron was scheduled for refresher carrier landings on an aircraft carrier which was enroute from San Diego to NAS Alameda in the San Francisco Bay area. Due to a shortage of aircraft, half of the pilots embarked on the carrier from San Diego; the other half flew out from Point Mugu to make their landings and remained on the carrier to Alameda. The group already on the ship made their landings and returned the aircraft to Mugu.

Lance made sure that he would be in the group continuing to San Francisco and had plans to meet a "friend" when the ship docked. His lady friend sent him a telegram saying something like, "Can't wait to see you! Have a room reserved for us at the Hyatt."

Unfortunately, the telegram arrived at the squadron after he flew out to the carrier and the squadron duty officer (who was not a pilot, and perhaps wasn't aware of the situation) called the pilot's home and delivered that message verbatim to the pilot's wife! When his buddies found out about this ill-timed notification, they sent an urgent radio message out to the ship.

Lance, never at a loss for brazen ideas, caught a commercial flight home from San Francisco, and somehow convinced his wife it was all her fault for driving him into the arms of another woman.

During a later assignment in Vietnam his career suffered a significant reversal when he was flying back from a night mission in an F-4 Phantom. He and his NFO received a message about another Phantom in trouble with a radio failure and could have been heroes. With help from the surface ships, they were able to navigate to the plane in distress, join up, and escort them back toward the carrier. However, they tuned in the wrong TACAN frequency and descended to a plane guard destroyer miles away from the carrier. Without enough fuel to climb back up and make an approach to the carrier, both planes had to fly alongside the destroyer and eject.

Apparently, their superiors took a dim view of their return without their airplanes, and I believe our hero was assigned to a radar site in Taiwan, a non-flying assignment. I later heard that he and his Taiwanese wife opened a very successful restaurant in L.A.

The Black Phantom

Someone at the Bureau had suggested we take a new look at camouflage. Our investigation had an aircraft painted with high gloss paint rather than the matte gray of most military aircraft. To our surprise the visual acquisition range was reduced by 75 percent, and in a head-on attack there were only seconds to maneuver against the oncoming aircraft. Paint color was also evaluated. Since the gloss paint reduced acquisition range, we decided to see if the critical element was color or gloss. We got one Phantom painted high gloss black to address the question, and found that gloss, not color was critical. When I did the first pre-flight after the black one came back from the paint shop, I noted my plane captain had painted "Black is Beautiful" on the back of the fuselage.

The Black Phantom.

The Black Phantom got a lot of attention on cross-country flights, since there were no other black aircraft out there, except for the SR-71.

During the hot summers, there tended to be long waits for transient aircraft needing fuel at military bases across the country. We would call from 100 miles out and ask for a sentry while the aircraft was on the ground. Because of the unique appearance of the black Phantom, the color, and the call for a sentry, we always got priority fueling. Bad behavior!

Woody and the Falcon

Kyle Woodbury, Woody, was a flamboyant aviator, and my boss for some time in the squadron. He was also a falconer and had one with which he hunted in the swamps on the base.

By way of background, capturing or killing a falcon was a serious federal offence as we found out when we called Woody later in D.C. for advice when my son rescued one and nursed it back to health after it crashed into our windbreak and injured a wing.

There was a federally sanctioned program for banding falcons to assess the population and their health. Woody asserted that there was a program in which he participated, in which they would catch, band, and release adult falcons, which required him and a helper. He tells this story:

> We did the banding at Assateague beach on an annual basis. It required setting up before dawn. The helper would bury me in the sand, with only my head showing, I was then covered with an inverted bushel basket with eye holes in it. A pigeon would be attached to a light string which was run through a pulley from my position back to where my helper hid in the marsh grass. The pigeon was then allowed to fly up, trailing the string.
>
> If a falcon spotted the pigeon and swooped down on it, their talons are like those of the eagle and can't release after striking until they land somewhere to deal with their prey. Thus, when a falcon struck, my helper could pull the string and haul it down. I would grab it, band the bird, and release it.
>
> After we were all set up and waiting, as the sun rose, a dune buggy suddenly appeared and headed down the beach toward us with a young couple aboard.
>
> Fortunately, they stopped before I had to think about removing the basket, so I remained still. To my surprise, they put down a blanket, took off their clothes, and frolicked a bit. After some spirited love making, they got up and wandered about, still naked, and the man started chucking pebbles at the basket!
>
> When he tired of that he came over and lifted up the basket. You can imagine his shock when he saw only a head in the sand. In a voice which a ghoul would have been proud of, I said "Put the basket back!" The couple then grabbed their clothes and blanket, threw them in the dune buggy, and roared away, still buck naked.

I never decided whether Woody experienced this, exaggerated it, or picked it up from somebody in the bar. It was better told with all the gestures and vocal expressions. Since he was, in fact, a licensed falconer and wild enough to participate in something like this, maybe it did happen!

NAS Glenview

Cross country navigation training was encouraged and for a guy who loved to fly that was next to going to heaven, but I nearly went the other way several times. One night flight to NAS Glenview near Chicago is worth mentioning. The only plane available was our old but trusty T-33 with limited navigation aids and no autopilot.

A ground officer from the squadron wanted me to drop him somewhere in Iowa and by the time the airplane was fueled, and back in the air, it was dark. Flying at night was fine but navigating in the clouds at night without an autopilot is tricky. The FAA flight controllers were very helpful but tended to change the planned route frequently due to traffic, weather, etc.

At 39,000 feet, it was solid instrument flight rules (IFR) and a bit bumpy. They gave me a change of route to some intersection I had never heard of. This led to a scramble to find the right nav chart, unfold it in the narrow cockpit, and find the intersection, with a flashlight in my mouth!

It was nice to finally see stars and be out of the clouds as I prepared to turn to the new course. However, the "stars" turned out to be the lights of Joliet, Illinois! With no autopilot, the aircraft had slowly entered a "death spiral," a gentle descending turn which provides no sense of motion to the pilot until the airplane was upside down and losing altitude quickly. Fortunately, there was no other traffic in the area and the altitude loss was only a couple of thousand feet. The flight ended with an uneventful instrument landing at the Naval Air Station, and a nice visit with my sister's family.

Low Level Air Show

We had some great air shows with military participation, as well as civilians like Bob Hoover and Art Scholl, among others. There was a crazy man whose name I can't remember, who flew a WWII twin engine/twin fuselage P-38 fighter inverted past the stands with both engines feathered. This was a plane which required a battery start. (And the airplane was notorious for battery problems.)

During the show, the P-38 pilot's wife <u>and</u> his mistress would sit together in the back seat of one of the Buick convertibles contributed for the show, feet draped over the front seat, watching his performance, and drinking martinis at 10:00am. I chatted with his wife later at a reception at the officers' club, and she mentioned they were having a "terrible" time finding a new home in Seattle, since they needed a lot large enough for a runway to accommodate his airplane!

One of my responsibilities was as an unofficial chauffeur for Bob Hoover, who flew to Mugu by helicopter from his office at North American Aviation in Los Angeles each day. During the show, he flew either a P-51 or a two-engine Shrike Commander which was an executive six-place airplane. My duties were to meet him at the ramp and take him to his plane, then return him later for the helicopter flight back to his office.

One of his most impressive maneuvers was doing a barrel roll with both engines feathered, while pouring iced tea into a glass resting on the instrument panel, then landing with both engines still feathered.

His military history was equally colorful. During the war he was shot down in Germany and was a POW for 11 months, before escaping by stealing a German fighter plane and landing safely in the Netherlands. He was reputed to be the best "stick and rudder" pilot in the world. He was also a real gentleman, without a hint of arrogance.

One year, the Blue Angels and the Thunderbirds were both in the same show and partying together. They were not up to their best the next day and one of the Blues flying an F-11 Tiger, their first plane with an afterburner, raised his gear too quickly on take-off and dragged the tail on the runway before getting in the air, turning the round afterburner into an oval!

In addition to the civilian stunt pilots, our squadron, as the host, put on a military demonstration. I was delighted to participate in the F-8 Crusader after some witty mechanic had painted a huge red cross on the fuselage.

One year the weather was terrible. The ceiling was even too low for the Blue Angels to do their "Low Show." Two of us were scheduled to demonstrate air-to-air refueling from a giant Air Force plane at 200 feet, while waiting for things to improve. Somebody later compared it to trying to fly formation on a city. We were orbiting below the clouds a bit inland, waiting to proceed so long that the low altitude air-to-air refueling at 200 feet was "for real," and not just a demonstration.

We were also scheduled for a low-level missile launch in front of the crowd to demonstrate the new Sidewinder missile, capable of reaching nearly Mach 2 with deadly accuracy against heat sources. The plan was to launch two missiles toward a parachute flare dropped by an antisubmarine airplane over the Santa Barbara Channel just offshore.

Nick Temple was leading our flight in a Phantom, and I was on his wing in a Crusader. As the bad weather continued, the show coordinator was getting desperate to show the audience something, since there were some 300,000 attendees during the weekend.

The first problem was that the S2F was out in the fog somewhere where we couldn't see it. They dropped the flare on time, but the parachute didn't open, and the flare went into the drink. The boss told us to launch anyway. The first Sidewinder went straight ahead at bush-top level with no heat source to home in on, and my missile went screaming after the first one.

The second problem was that there was a lone Marine out there in the swamp, tending a fire in a 55-gallon oil drum which was supposed have something to do with a simulated atomic bomb blast. The missiles suddenly acquired that heat source, and we could see them suddenly change course, blasting through a large data tracking van at desktop level. Fortunately, they blew up a bridge short of the hapless Marine and his oil drum.

Nello and the $293,000 Bill

Shortly after the air show I was doing the annual medical exam for the admiral who was the C.O. of the base and missile range. He and Nello were golfing buddies. He told me that there had been $293,000 damage from the missile shoot and confided that he was going to play a joke on Nello.

Nello was a gung-ho, fun-loving guy, but very protective of his troops, our flying, and our reputation. Soon, both Nick and I were called to the C.O.'s office. Nello was fuming about the letter from the admiral, who stated that the show was enjoyable, but that the squadron would have to pay $293,000 for the damage.

The only place we could get that kind of money was from the fuel budget; Nello had quickly figured out that we would be essentially grounded for three months with no fuel. He called us both to the office and after reading us the riot act for some time, he dismissed us still fretting over the fate of the squadron.

Standing at attention during the diatribe and recalling the conversation with the admiral, an idea came to mind to calm Nello and let him know it was a joke. I went down the hall to my office, dug out my Navy lieutenant's Bank of Pensacola checkbook, penned a check for $293,000, and dropped it on the C.O.'s desk. Nello was used to playing pranks, not having them played on him, but after realizing what had happened, he took it in good spirits. The framed check remained on the wall for as long as I was there.

A Night Project at China Lake

One of the more intriguing projects involved a test of the Sidewinder heat seeking missile, modified to seek light sources at night rather than heat sources. The seeker head was extremely sensitive; we were told at NAS Miramar in San Diego during the briefing that the seeking head could home in on a porch light at three miles! The planned modification was to have a light seeking missile which could pick up the headlight from a locomotive in a tunnel, where the North Vietnamese tended to park them during the night to evade radar. The headlight would be a pretty good target for the modified Sidewinder.

For our evaluation, a missile light sensing head only was mounted on the wing of a Phantom. The profile established for the test included three dives, at 15 degrees, 30 degrees, and 45 degrees, locking onto a porch light or similar light source, starting at 5000 feet above ground, at a speed of 450 knots, and pulling out at 2000 feet.

One has to expect that things don't always go as planned, especially at night. It was one of those rare times when there were clouds down to 4000 feet above ground along Highway 395 in the desert.

To establish the dive and acquire a target, it was necessary to pull up into the clouds, roll over, set the dive angle, and find a target. That didn't allow much time for tracking or safe pullout from the dive.

The NFO in the back seat was operating the navigation gear and tasked with calling off the altitude in the dive to me. My job was to find a target and fly the profile with the guy in back monitoring the altitude and calling us off at 3000 feet.

Bridgham and Black Phantom.

The first two approaches were smooth due to the comparatively shallow dives, and the acquisition of targets was easy in the dive. The night was dark enough that the pull-out altitude was critical for safety reasons since there was no ground reference except for the occasional porch light or automobile. I was concentrating on target acquisition and proper dive angle and counting on my back seat guy to count down the altitude.

All was going well in the 45-degree dive until I glanced momentarily at the altimeter, to see it spinning through 1700 feet. The emergency pull-up in afterburner probably exceeded the established 9G limit for the airplane and caused momentary black-out of vision for both of us. As my sight came back, I saw high tension power lines whizzing by on our left, which put us right over the highway.

Apparently, we were saved by sinking briefly into an arroyo. As the airplane began to recover two automobile headlights suddenly came over the rise. It turns out the NFO was watching the radar slant range to the target, rather than the altimeter. We always wondered what the driver said as these two giant plumes of flame washed overhead only a few feet above him. Probably some good stories at cocktail hour in L.A. Another "Shoulda been dead."

High Altitude Accident

For several months during the summer (always on weekends) the flight surgeon (me) was assigned to fly to San Nicholas Island 60 miles south of Point Mugu, to stand by for possible rescue duties unrelated to the squadron, involving some high-altitude project for which the managers would provide no details other than that the pilot(s) had conventional ejection seats. I was restricted from the briefing, but the planners did leave chalk board drawings indicating a flight passing over Point Mugu, accelerating from there to the vicinity of Wake Island, then circling south to somewhere off the South American coast in 90 minutes, which would suggest a distance of 6000 miles at a speed of Mach 4 to Mach 6!

Later there were additional details, indicating the "vehicle," whatever it was, would pass over Point Mugu at a speed of Mach 3 at 80,000 feet. There was speculation that it was a souped-up SR-71 or the mysterious "Aurora," thought to be another plane in development at the "Skunk Works" in Palmdale, and perhaps flown out of the facility at Groom Lake and rumored to be capable of Mach 6. These were all fragmentary bits of information, gathered both before and after the event.

The rescue helicopter carried us to San Nicholas Island, 60 miles south, and we anticipated another dull Saturday on a deserted island looking skyward. After a quiet morning, we suddenly got the call for the helicopter to get underway for an emergency rescue. The low clouds characteristic of the season over the Santa Barbara Channel were just beginning to clear, but we readily found the missile range boat. The helicopter pilot noted that their stability augmentation system wasn't working, and they couldn't lower me onto the small boat rocking in the mild sea. I spotted an inert figure in a silver space suit lying on the deck, and perhaps without enough thought, I told them to drop me and the Stevenson rescue kit into the water, since it was a short swim to the boat. When the sailors pulled me aboard, one commented, "Doc, that was the bravest thing I ever saw!" It seemed excessive praise for a 30-yard swim until he added, "Didn't you see all the sharks out there?" Another "Shoulda been dead!"

The aviator was not responsive, even when the crew picked him out of the water earlier and he was beyond resuscitation. Another serious problem arose shortly thereafter when a fire erupted in the engine compartment, which was located just below the hatch where the inert aviator was lying. The crewmen were initially reluctant to try to drag away a dead man above a fire. He was a big man, but we were finally able to get him clear of the involved hatch cover.

When the fire was controlled, we found ourselves stranded 60 miles from shore. Late in the afternoon we got a tow from another range boat and slowly made our way back to Mugu. The pilot of the aircraft had ejected, landed unscathed, and arrived at Mugu long before we did. He departed in a four-engine Constellation for debriefing wherever he came from; I never met him. There was a second Connie waiting for the second crew member. We surmised that the vehicle exploded above 80,000 feet, already above Mach 3 in the acceleration phase, so this was probably the highest, fastest successful ejection on record.

At high altitudes, aircraft ejection seats are automatically stabilized by a small drogue chute programmed to descend quickly, while the oxygen tank in the seat pack pressurizes the space suit and provides breathing oxygen until the seat reaches 12,000 feet. At that point, the occupant is detached from the seat and the main chute opens.

The first pilot depended on the automatic system, which worked as programmed. We assumed that the other pilot, unable to see the ocean due to the low clouds, elected to manually separate from the seat at a high altitude, where the oxygen supply was required to keep the space suit pressurized and to provide oxygen for breathing. Due to the slower rate of descent when he deployed his chute manually, he ran out of oxygen, became unconscious, and drowned before he could be picked up.

The project was so highly classified that I wasn't allowed even to notify the admiral at Mugu, leaving me to try to deal with Air Force generals in Washington.

We transferred the deceased flyer to the dispensary, which had limited security or privacy. Kids were peeking around the drapes at the man in the silver space suit. My plan was to put the man on the second Connie and return him to where he came from, since he died in international waters, and nobody officially knew he was at Mugu.

At this point bureaucracy trumped common sense, and we were told that our man would not be removed from his gear.

By state law, a dead person could not be taken from the county until cleared by the coroner, so our top-secret pilot was transferred to a mortuary in Oxnard, still in his space suit, with a tag on his toe saying "John Doe," although his name was written on the inside of his boots. We got authorization to move him to his home base the following morning on the Constellation. A sad day.

ECEIVES NAVY COMMENDATION MEDAL — Dr. William H. Browning III, lieutenant in the U.S. Medical Corps and son of Dr. and Mrs. William H. rowning of Morgan Street, is shown as the award is pinned during ceremon-is held recently at the Naval Air Station, Point Mugu, Calif. (U.S. Navy Photo)

t. Browning Cited for Heroism

INT MUGU, Calif. — Dr. am H. Browning III, U.S. cal Corps lieutenant and one medical officers in the e U.S. Navy who has Naval or Wings, was cited recently ie Naval Air Station here warded the Navy Commenda-

tion Medal for heroism on July 30, 1966 while serving at this Naval Air Station.

Dr. Browning, son of Dr. and Mrs. William H. Browning of Morgan Street, Bennington, is presently attached to the Air Development Squadron Four, which is involved in the test and evaluation of Naval aircraft and weapons systems. Presently he flies the F5B Phantom II and the F-8 Crusader.

The citation signed by Paul H. Nitze, Secretary of the Navy, which accompanied the medal reads: "For heroism on 30 July 1966 while serving at the Naval Air Station, Point Mugu, California. Upon receiving a request

a Pacific Missile Range AVR rescue boat, Lieutenant Browning proceeded by helicopter to the scene, approximately 35 miles south of San Nicolas Island.

"With the rough sea making a normal transfer from the helicopter to the boat impossible, the helicopter then maneuvered to a point about 15 yards from the boat where Lieutenant Browning dropped into the water from a height of 10 to 15 feet. Although the water was extremely rough, he swam to the AVR rescue boat, climbed aboard and proceeded to administer aid to the injured aircrewman. By his prompt and courageous action in the face of personal dan

Commendation Medal.

Quonset Point

In 1967, VX-4 sent a temporary detachment from NAS Quonset Point to test advanced electronic countermeasures (ECM) systems in our warplanes to better evade the fire control radar of the North Vietnamese. A SAM missile installation had been set up in the White Mountains of New Hampshire for testing the effectiveness of new systems in our airplanes. The project required three pilots and a RIO (Radar Intercept Officer). Gary Hakanson, Mike Welch, and I were the pilots; Phil Anselmo was the RIO. We had two airplanes, an F-4 Phantom and an F-8 Crusader. Gary was qualified in the Phantom and Mike in the Crusader, and I was qualified in both. There was also a detachment of skilled enlisted men to keep the airplanes flying.

At one point, the Phantom was "down" for parts we didn't have. Considering the high priority of the project, we needed to get that fixed ASAP. Mike, the other Crusader pilot, was up in New Hampshire coordinating communications for the tests and we were trying to find a solution, since there were no parts for jets at Quonset. The chief of maintenance called around to his buddies and found the needed part at Cherry Point Marine Corps Air Station in North Carolina. The weather was not favorable since it was a stormy night in Rhode Island, and we were in Hurricane

Condition One for a storm roaring up the coast. The leaders back at the home squadron decided to send me to Cherry Point anyway.

As one could imagine, the prospects were a bit daunting. As I was taxiing out for take-off and getting IFR clearance from New York Center, several things were notable. First, it was dark, raining, and the wind was blowing large stuff around on the taxiways. Second, all the other airplanes on base were safely locked up inside the hangars. Not a big confidence builder.

Fuel wasn't a problem, and I asked for an unrestricted climb to try to get above the weather; New York Center cheerfully answered, "Permission granted – you're the only one out there!"

The F-8 Crusader had a great climb rate in afterburner, with the altimeter winding up so fast that it passed through 55,000 feet before I could roll over and get back down to the assigned altitude.

It was clear above the storm, with a beautiful moonlit night above the clouds. The route was directly over New York City, which was at the eye of the storm, and looking down through that eye of the storm at the lights of the city was quite remarkable.

The rest of the trip was one of those night flights where you can't imagine a better place to be. It was still raining in North Carolina but the approach wasn't difficult. They gave me the part we needed, as well as a bed, and the return flight was much less exciting.

Red Horse

Our squadron, VX-4, had quarterly mandatory "Dining-In Celebrations," which were dinner dances in military formal uniforms and gowns for the ladies. One of my jobs was to mold hundreds of plastic Navy Wings, which were painted gold and pinned to blue fabric "walls" of the officers' club as souvenirs for all.

Those parties always included toasts to the C.O., the Secretary of the Navy, the President, and Heads of Service for any exchange pilots, and so on.

There were usually skits put on by some of our squadron members, and often they were quite good. One was a spoof on the TV program "Laugh In" which included a pilot on a tricycle that always tipped over.

At that time the base commander was a former Naval Academy fullback nicknamed "Red Horse." He was still a big man, and a bit of a drinker. We fashioned a "social crutch" for him, which was a wooden crutch decked out with a bicycle light (to help him find his way home), a soap dish to hold his drink, and a bicycle bell to summon the barmaid (frequently). After the presentation, in his speech of thanks, he unfortunately included the following, "If any of you had a hair on your ass, you would try to steal this thing!"

At that, the party descended into chaos and a serious effort to steal the crutch began. This eventually included ripping the door off the ready liquor locker behind the bar. That occasioned a call to base security and the shore patrol.

I was quite sober and left to go to our home on base for bolt cutters, with the idea of shutting off the electric power to lessen the mayhem. When I re-entered the club, our Air Force exchange officer and another pilot were engaged in banter with Red Horse, ready to push him over, and another was on all fours behind him. As he fell, they grabbed the crutch and tossed it to me. Red Horse was quite nimble, for a large man with too much alcohol, and he sprinted after me as I fled the club.

The "Black Shoes" (Naval officers who were not in the aviation community) and their wives were hurrying away from this unseemly brawl, and the couple ahead of me let the door swing shut just as I got there and crashed through the plate glass. I eluded capture, but ended up winded, lying in the sand on the beach behind the club with multiple lacerations to face and hands. The sleeve of my jacket was cut nearly to the skin at the shoulder, hanging down over the bleeding hand.

A sailor with the Shore Patrol was standing by his truck as I made my way to my car, hatless and looking a bit like somebody from a bloody horror movie. His only reaction was to salute smartly, and say something like "Have a nice evening, sir!" I made my way to the dispensary to be sewn up. The doctor on duty was an Internist named Vic, who paled at the sight of blood, and that led to the following story.

Vic at Mach 2

One of the more fanciful projects was to evaluate the possibility of shooting down an intercontinental ballistic missile (ICBM) from a Phantom, which required reaching an altitude of 70,000 feet and using a space suit. Because of the aeromedical aspects of flying in space suits, I was assigned to develop the profiles to achieve that altitude. A space suit was required since a loss of pressurization above 55,000 feet without a suit meant instant death, since blood boils at body temperature at that altitude. Okay, so it was still fun.

For the maneuver, the aircraft had to climb to 45,000 feet, then dive to 20,000 feet in afterburner to achieve Mach 2, followed by a climb to maximum altitude. The run had to be made over the Santa Barbara Channel to avoid the sonic boom over land, and at the end of the run usually ended up 100 miles west of Vandenberg AFB in a low fuel state.

The Phantom loses all control response above 60,000 feet and becomes a rock. The computer backs off the engines to idle so they won't flame out. The maximum I achieved was 69,000 feet, where the sky is black, and one can see the curvature of the earth. That is a thrilling sight!

Lt. Browning and his Phantom.

Often the airplane will stay in the attitude it was when the controls became ineffective, or sometimes it will fall off on one wing, out of control, until it falls to around 50,000 feet, where the wings regain some "bite."

Every effort was made not to end up backing down, since the reverse air flow could blow out the afterburners, and a two-engine air start was a "sometimes" thing.

At that point, the airplane was about a hundred miles out and at low fuel state since we couldn't go supersonic with external fuel tanks.

The Phantom didn't glide very well, but at that altitude had minimum fuel consumption in the glide back toward home. That was the good thing; the bad thing was that Mugu was often fogged in, even in the daytime, and there was only enough fuel left for one approach. The GCA (ground-controlled approach) guys were really great and got me home even with 200-foot ceilings and low fuel.

Because of the nature of these flights, a guy in the back seat wasn't needed for the practice runs. If we got to the "real" launch, he would be there for target acquisition

Vic, the doc who sewed up my many lacerations from the officers' club fiasco, wanted a flight in the Phantom in return. He was a really nice guy but didn't look like he favored the California sun; tall, lanky, and always pale. He went through all the ground training required, including the low-pressure chamber and the ejection seat. Because the NFO was not required for these flights, permission was granted to take Vic along.

On that fateful day, we suited up normally since we weren't going above 50,000 feet. I made every effort to make it like a commercial flight, with gentle turns and a cruise climb. Despite those efforts, before we even departed from the field boundary, Vic said, "Bill, I don't feel so good."

I encouraged him to get his head out of the cockpit and admire his home in base housing as we passed over it. We climbed on course over Disneyland and turned toward Catalina, with me as the (unsuccessful) tour guide.

Vic had the distinction of being the only person I ever knew who barfed over Disneyland, over Catalina, at Mach 2, and on landing roll out. By that time his barf bag was full, as was his helmet. The crew chief dodged the unpleasant liquid dribbling from his helmet after we parked and climbed out. As we walked back across the tarmac Vic said, "Bill, I want you to know this was the best day of my life!" It was hard to imagine what might have been his worst.

Have Donut

A Russian pilot defected to Israel in a MiG-21, and the separate acquisition of a MiG-17 gave us a unique opportunity to study the capabilities of those aircraft against our fighters. The task was coordinated between our squadron and Air Force pilots from Nellis AFB in Las Vegas flying both the MiGs and the American fighters.

The project was highly classified, and only a few of our pilots were allowed access. The Russian planes were hangared at Groom Lake to avoid satellite surveillance, and the project flights conducted over the restricted Site 51 area.

Extremely valuable information was gained about the capabilities of both Russian airplanes, which was subsequently passed on by our project pilots to squadrons deploying to Vietnam. Those lectures were later integrated into the "Top Gun" program at Miramar.

My only access to the program or the area was when we lost a Phantom after it had a double engine flame-out during a zero-speed reversal at low altitude in exercises against the MiG. I was taken by helicopter to the accident site as part of the accident investigation. Cockpit voice communications were all captured by telemetry and listening to the conversation was chilling. The crew reported the flame-out at 8000 feet, and repeated efforts to start one or both engines were unsuccessful. In a remarkably cool voice, the pilot discussed the ejection sequence with the RIO and finally told him to get out, and then further delayed ejecting until the last possible minute.

He survived unscathed, and I found his boot skid marks barely two feet from the crater made by the completely destroyed aircraft, of which little remained except a few engine parts in the desert. Later, someone with tongue in cheek had painted a little Phantom near the canopy rail of the MiG, to record the "kill."

Tacoma Cross Country Flight

I was scheduled for an IFR cross-country training flight to McChord AFB in Tacoma, Washington, on a Saturday. The distance was around 800 nautical miles, well within range for the Crusader.

In that time, weather briefings and clearances had to be delivered on paper to operations. Perhaps the yeoman stopped for coffee along the way and that, combined with fueling problems, delayed take-off for several hours.

Once in the air, the weather had changed from the original forecast to a 100-mph headwind, which forced a quick recalculation of fuel requirements. There was still sufficient fuel to get to the destination, or to divert to Spokane if the weather was below minimums at McChord. At about 100 miles from the destination, the forecast was a 3000-foot ceiling and 3-mile visibility in light rain.

That was well above Navy minimums requiring diversion to an alternate, so I started the let-down into Tacoma under FAA control. The Navy minimum for an approach in bad weather is a 200-foot ceiling, and one-half-mile visibility.

I was familiar with the terrain around McChord and expected to see forests at 3000-foot altitude. Not so. Nothing at 2000, or 1000, where I got really focused on the ground-controlled approach (GCA), which is the approach made with the navigation instruments in the cockpit, supplemented with heading and glide slope guidance from a radar controller at the field.

At this point it was getting dark, and worse, the BIG red low-fuel warning light came on, meaning that the airplane had to land on this pass, or it would be necessary to climb up as far as possible, and eject over Puget Sound. Serious problem!

After reaching an altitude of 90 feet without seeing the runway in sight, I started to wave-off, when suddenly one runway light flashed past at 6000 feet down the runway. By then, the aircraft had accelerated to about 240 knots, but the only choice was to force it back onto the ground, where it fishtailed at least 30 degrees left and right on the wet runway, finally stopping with the intake over the end of the concrete.

The tower told me to taxi to the transient area, but nothing was visible in the fog, so they had to send a "follow me" truck, which got me to transient parking.

The post-flight procedure for this aircraft required checking the oil from the top of the fuselage immediately after shut-down. If one tries to achieve that in the dark in sleet and rain, usually a fall of about 10 feet results, as was the case that night. I got the wind knocked out of me, and icy water down the back of the winter flight suit. The old civilian fuel truck driver hobbled over and asked, "Do you want me to call a doctor?" My response, "G–damn it, I am a doctor!" still sounds ridiculous.

Angry about the lousy weather report, I confronted the meteorologist, who was sitting with his feet on the deck, coffee in hand. When I exploded, his casual response was, "The weather report was based on looking north." This made no sense at all since all the approaches were from the south. One more "Shoulda been dead."

Phil's Wedding

Phil was the only bachelor among the fliers in the squadron at the time. He was a really good RIO, great to work and fly with, always ready to laugh, and who took ribbing in stride. Near the end of his tour, he met a lovely girl, became engaged, and we all kidded him about how in the world she would put up with him. A formal Navy wedding was planned, in dress whites with swords, and all the pomp and circumstance involved.

His fellow officers decided he deserved a rousing bachelor party before the wedding, and some of the mischief was determined to be my responsibility. His so-called buddies got him quite drunk, and he finally passed out. Then the really mean mischief began, and a story was hatched to later tell him he had fallen into the base swimming pool, which had been emptied for the season, and sustained an ankle injury requiring a cast. I was tasked with applying a cast with some small irritant in it to create ankle pain. His "friends" then obtained some gentian violet, an old-fashioned treatment for fungal infections, and painted him from knees to chest with the dark purple liquid.

The cast was removed by the wedding day, but the gentian violet was not so easy to remove. Fortunately, it did not bleed through his dress whites. He and his bride left on honeymoon shortly thereafter, before I could pass on the information about how to remove the pesky purple stain.

Phil went on to become an admiral, and was the Wing Commander at Miramar, the first NFO to achieve that level of command. I figured I better retire before he demoted me!

Aviator Flight Surgeons

During the '60s and '70s, there was category of "dual designated" Navy Flight Surgeons who were also Naval Aviators. The original twelve of us were all aviators who had gotten out of the Navy, attended medical school, then returned, graduated from the School of Aerospace Medicine in Pensacola, and went through refresher flight training for assignment to a billet where we took on medical duties for their squadron as well as flying assignments requiring medical or biological expertise. There was one assigned to the Marines, and the rest to the large, advanced training bases including Whidbey Island in the Seattle area, Miramar in San Diego, Oceana in Virginia, Patuxent River in Maryland, Jacksonville in Florida, and VX-4 at Point Mugu.

Later, the Navy began accepting Flight Surgeons with no aviation experience to undergo the full flight training syllabus. Some of us were not enthusiastic about that for good reason.

A study at the school in Pensacola had a surprising outcome which showed that even those physicians with a stated interest in going through the School of Aviation Medicine program had poorer "flight aptitude ratings" than an unselected group of college students.

Some of these students were moved along through training even though they did not have favorable high ratings from their instructors. A group of flight instructors kept a log indelicately called the "Bust Your Ass" book, and their poor flight aptitude ratings were strongly correlated with a high mortality rate at three years out.

My theory was that the mindset of someone enduring the arduous medical school program resulted in a know-it-all attitude, at odds with that of an aviator. If the Landing Signal Officer says "power, power, power!" as a plane approaches the rear of the carrier, the aviator adds power without question, whereas the doctor is apt to think "why is he telling me to do that?" with a very bad outcome.

After the informal previous in-house selection of the first scientist astronaut, a more structured selection process was adopted for the batch of 1875 applicants. We heard that the screening was to be performed by the National Academy of Science, and that did not deal with flight aptitude or flight experience. I was screened out with 23 applicants remaining. Eventually 11 or 12 were selected, none of whom had military flight experience. It was later reported that five were killed during basic flight training, and six more resigned based on the mortality rate.

Superhero

When my assignment to VX-4 was nearing an end with an anticipated transfer to Patuxent River, the doctor scheduled to replace me was one of the dual-designates who got his flight training after med school. He flew in to Mugu from Florida, ostensibly to familiarize himself with the squadron and his duties.

He arrived at Mugu in an A-4, a jet fighter/attack aircraft. The A-4 had a centerline external fuel tank which had been converted to a baggage carrier, in which he carried his clothes. He neglected to fasten the latch of the tank before take-off. All of his baggage was sucked out and scattered over the Everglades, and he arrived with only the unusual silver flight suit he was wearing. He said he was evaluating that for the Navy, but he looked a bit more like Elvis Presley or a Superhero. After a brief hello, he left in a rental car to see a nurse friend in Los Angeles. Two days later he called to ask if I would drive to L.A. to bring him some clothes. We were about the same size, and the silver flight suit routine apparently was getting old.

My family was returning from Japan on a commercial flight to Los Angeles the same day and I readily agreed. When I found the apartment, he was celebrating with two or three very attractive young nurses, drinking French 75s, a potent mix of champagne and brandy, at ten in the morning.

He then had me chauffeur him to a liquor store for a refill. It was quite odd to see him in his unique silver flight suit walking the streets of L.A. When we got back to the apartment where his nurse friend lived, I was pleased to find the conversations much more substantive than one might expect in this situation.

With a bit of time left before needing to get to the airport to pick up the family. I got involved in a debate about something, then realized the plane with my wife and three small children was arriving shortly at LAX.

I made a hasty exit and raced down Hollywood Boulevard at 60 mph, hoping not to see a patrol car along the way, arriving just in time. As usual, there was a huge traffic jam at the airport, I abandoned the car in traffic at the terminal, and made it just as the kids were running down the exit ramp. I don't know why my car wasn't towed; I guess we got back before the traffic had progressed two or three car lengths, and people just expected it to be that way.

Eventually Captain America arrived back at Point Mugu, returned my clothes (still rumpled) and departed, no wiser about the job than when he arrived.

Epilogue: As mentioned, attitude and experience are valuable. My relief got disoriented on a night instrument landing at Point Mugu and crashed, killing himself and his RIO, a good friend of mine.

Nello and Marcia

The Pierozzis remained friends for life, and frequently joined us at the condo in Mammoth for skiing. I remember Marcia used to make pointed remarks about "dummy bumps" if I strayed out of the lane on 395, because sometimes they rode up with us and sometimes rode in Nello's favorite Toyota Celica. Nello always did 100 sit-ups, pushups, and jumping jacks before breakfast, and was in excellent shape.

I think Marcia wasn't as enthusiastic about skiing as Nello, who was a very pretty skier, and who dragged me onto trails a bit above my comfort level. He was always flirting with the young girls at the base of the lifts and would start conversations with strangers in the main lodge. He also loaded his pockets with Equal or sugar when he got coffee and when I would chide him about "stealing" he always retorted that they were there for the taking.

One cold snowy morning during one of our frequent pauses for coffee, he marched up to an elderly couple and asked them how old they were. Then he went on about how great it was for them to be skiing in their 80s, and free at that. He liked free.

One time, when we were snowed in, I remember Nello on the couch, with his feet stretched out in front of him, remarking on an article that fascinated him in the Reader's Digest magazine. It was an article on flatulence, which was of particular interest to him, since he has an amazing ability to add noise and gases to global warming. The article mentioned something about the average frequency of passing gas, and he remarked that he had already used up his quota for 20 or 30 years to come.

Good times with the Pierozzis.

He also had unwittingly created a new nickname for one of their friends. A group of us were lounging in his living room in San Diego and Nello was sitting on the couch next to one of Marcia's friends. He had his arm over her shoulder, massaging the shoulder pad on her dress. She had an odd expression, and Marcia and I, sitting opposite them, were astonished, since he was unconsciously massaging her breast. He was highly embarrassed, and forever after, that lady was known as "Shoulders."

With the idea of continuing the quest for the astronaut program, Nello encouraged me to apply to the Test Pilot School (TPS) at Patuxent River. It was expected that I would relieve Bill Crawford, the current Aviator Flight Surgeon at TPS. As soon as we arrived, Bill took me up for a "recon" flight over potential homes near the base and we picked a very nice home in a wooded area close to town, near a pool for the kids. Odd way to pick a home!

While waiting to start the TPS program, there was very limited flying available, no guy in the back seat of the Phantom, and a very small operating area up and down Chesapeake Bay compared with the Pacific Missile Range. There was no opportunity to tangle with Air Force pilots for air combat exercises.

The base had a real hospital, rather than a dispensary, and the C.O. was a real doctor and a good boss. The hospital was able to manage out-patient surgeries and recoveries.

A memorable bit of surgery for me was a minor procedure on my good friend stationed in D.C., who wanted to "have his tubes tied" (a vasectomy). Usually that is a short procedure done with local anesthesia, finding the tubes carrying the sperm just under the skin, cutting and tying them off. Simple, right?

He drove down for the procedure one evening, which was completed in a few minutes without incident, and he drove back the same night. As soon as he got home, though, I got a call asking "What the Hell! I drove back with a basketball between my legs." Apparently, a small bleeder erupted after the skin was closed. Fortunately, there was no long-term damage to the patient or the friendship.

There was one tragedy which remains fresh in memory. A fellow physician at the hospital with surgical training did most of the elective cases. One night the C.O. alerted me that my colleague's wife, six months pregnant, had a pulmonary embolus and was unresponsive. He rushed her to the hospital, found resuscitation was not possible, and made the terrible choice to operate on his dead wife to try to save the baby. Sadly, to no avail.

Course Change

The three-month wait to start the test pilot class turned out to be fortunate rather than tedious. My predecessor briefed me on the program and likely career progression, and we made visits to the "big guys" in D.C.

It was increasingly evident that the duty assignments for aviator flight surgeons involved less and less flying, less and less medicine, and apparently more and more alcohol. Not really an enviable career path.

The C.O. at the hospital was a good physician, leader, and counselor. He discussed available options, knew about my interest in orthopedics, and found that there was a vacancy in the training program at the Chelsea Naval Hospital in Boston.

I was accepted for that slot in the training program, and we ended up moving even before the purchase of the house was finalized.

Cross-country camping with the family.

Our transfers were always fraught with something unexpected. Before we departed, the universal joint on our station wagon needed replacement, and the work was done inside the garage since the late fall season was chilly.

The car was on a ramp, with the parking brake set and the transmission in "park." Bad plan! When the universal joint was disconnected, the transmission was no longer connected to the universal joint in back, and the parking brake was not enough to stop the car from rolling off the ramp, and partially through the garage door of the home we hadn't bought yet. It was fixable but didn't help to expedite our transfer to Boston and Orthopedic residency.

BOSTON

Boston and Chelsea Naval Hospital

On the north shore of the Mystic River, Chelsea Naval Hospital had originally been an ammunition storage site during the Civil War and showed signs of wear. The dependents' ward was in another building that was connected by a tunnel under a cross street. The ceiling of the tunnel tended to leak on the bed as the patient was wheeled to the operating room. The enlisted ward in the main building had broken screens, no air conditioning, and a broken outdoor stair railing, which posed a real challenge for a patient on crutches during icy weather.

The chief of orthopedics at Chelsea was a man well loved and respected in the Navy orthopedic community, and a good teacher. However, we did not know that he was moving to San Diego shortly, leaving us with a very small department with four residents, and teaching limited to two career guys and two doctors from the "Berry Plan." They all did make real efforts to provide a good training experience.

At that time (1970) we were overwhelmed with 36 enlisted men in a ward which was a converted WWII barracks. Most were returning from Vietnam with terrible wounds, and much of our work was skin grafts for burns and blast injuries and some amputations.

Restorative surgery was limited at that time, since bone rods, sophisticated plates, and joint replacements were in their infancy, and infection was a great risk with the antibiotics available at the time. Towels were limited to one a week for those bed-ridden in traction.

Due to the woeful lack of sanitary conditions, we had problems with maggots in the wounds. The Chief was making rounds with us one morning. We were astonished to see migrating red drops on the bed sheets of a man with multiple areas of skin loss. His skin grafts were dressed with Scarlet Red, used in that day as a bactericidal paint. The red drops turned out to be maggots which had picked up the red color from the dressing and were marching away from the wound and dropping off the edge of the bed! Wonder what the JCAH (The Joint Commission on Accreditation of Hospitals) would have to say about that these days?

Along with wonderful nurses, there was a Navy Corpsman assisting me. He was from Massachusetts, and he said that his father was a doctor in Pittsfield. He was an interesting fellow, a rehab patient too, who had shot himself in the foot accidentally at the end of his duty in Vietnam.

He told hair-raising stories about men on patrol, many of whom were stoned on drugs, and the village kids who traipsed along begging for gum, but were suspiciously absent on days when the patrol was to be hit by the Viet Cong.

He was a good assistant and a church organ enthusiast, familiar with most of the famous installations in the world. He introduced me to the organ music played by E. Power Biggs, whom he called "Biggie."

In all this misery of the mangled young men, there was at least one humorous incident. Our boss had reasoned that if he could get Ted Kennedy to visit the ward, the senator would have the horsepower to improve the woeful state of affairs for our patients.

This was shortly after the tragedy in Martha's Vineyard, when Kennedy left a party with a 28-year-old woman named Mary Jo Kopechne in his Oldsmobile. The sedan veered off a narrow bridge at Chappaquiddick and landed upside down in a pond. Kennedy was able to escape through a window and swim to shore, but was unable to extricate his passenger, who drowned.

Senator Kennedy arrived with the C.O. of the hospital and a TV news cinematographer in tow. He was obviously searching for a good photo op, but when he surveyed all the young men with scraggly hair, beards, peace symbol tattoos, and no chance for return to duty, there weren't many likely prospects. He finally spotted the only well-groomed man on the ward, in bed with one arm and one leg in casts.

Senator Kennedy and Dr. Browning.

The young petty officer in question was assigned to a secret surveillance unit on Nantucket, near Martha's Vineyard. After a night of poker and alcohol, he failed to negotiate a T-intersection on his motorcycle sustaining the injuries requiring hospitalization.

To my horror, Mr. Kennedy and his retinue approached him, and said something along the lines of, "Well, son, did you get your injuries in the war?" The young man replied, "No sir, I was involved in a motor vehicle accident on Nantucket." Someone in the large group murmured, loud enough to be heard by everyone, "Yeah, you know, Senator, the roads are pretty narrow out there." Thus ended the interview and our hopes for screens and air conditioning.

One patient worth forgetting was a man who rolled a grenade underneath his C.O.'s hut in Vietnam and was in a military prison in New Hampshire.

He burned off both hands while trying to escape from prison by climbing down a steam pipe which ruptured. He was most unwelcome throughout. He masqueraded as a master sergeant in the Marine Corps and played on the sympathy of the young ladies in town. The final injustice was when the authorities in New Hampshire gave him a new car equipped for handicapped drivers!

At the beginning of our four years in Boston, we bought a just-completed home in Danvers, in the north suburbs, and had time to build a back deck and post and rail fence, design a Japanese garden with a stone staircase, and plant glorious roses, The neighbors were very friendly and welcoming. The schools were good, and our three children enjoyed them. We also enjoyed the nearby lobsters and good ice cream.

Willy, Bill, Michael, Sadako, and Suzie.

The training experience was divided between a definitely "hands on" experience at Chelsea, and rotation through the Peter Bent Brigham Hospital, with leaders in the rapidly expanding use of joint replacements and metal fixation of fractures. We were exposed to conferences and lectures by the leading orthopedists in the world, as well as assisting in the O.R.

Happy times at the beach.

Dr. John Hall

The other wonderful opportunity was a year at Boston Children's Hospital with Dr. John Hall, felt by many to be the leading children's orthopedic surgeon in the world and perhaps the best teacher as well. He was a meticulous surgeon, a perfectionist, and a quiet giant in the field, with a subtle wit. When he first arrived in Boston from Toronto, he was invited to give an address to the prestigious local orthopedic society.

His opening comment was, "It is a great pleasure to be in Boston, a city with a history of 186 years of orthopedics, untrammeled by progress."

I was fortunate to have enough time in the O.R. with him that he was willing to let me do a complex spine operation by myself while he was out of town.

Ruth, his O.R. nurse, was a great help introducing the trainees to the "toolboxes" full of orthopedic instruments and implants. She always had a ready laugh. We became good friends and she even brought her talents and trays to Bethesda later to help me with a complex spine case.

The other luminaries teaching us were Ted Riseborough and Hugh Watts, both also from Toronto. Ted was a colorful British guy who built a large sailboat in his garage and towed it through the city streets to its berth in the harbor. Hugh was a great hands-on mentor as well, with a wicked sense of humor.

The four years sped by too quickly and with orthopedic training finished, we got orders to Bethesda, where they needed an urgent replacement for Al Crawford, the pediatric orthopedist when he transferred to the Naval Hospital in San Diego. I was pleased that Al and I frequently crossed paths during his career as surgeon, lecturer, and teacher.

Boston to Bethesda

The transfer from Boston to Bethesda was my first assignment as a children's orthopedist. The three children, Suzie (11), Willy (8), and Michael (7), were looking forward to the neighborhood outdoor swim club after the chilly years in Boston. We had two cars to transfer; my Mercury Cougar, just repainted due to the damage from three years of road salt, as well as our trusty Plymouth station wagon with its large car top carrier. My wife Sadako did not favor freeway driving but did a great job of following the Cougar in the station wagon, through New York traffic, and through a deluge so heavy around Baltimore that most cars had to stop along the freeway.

Triumphantly through that, we were approaching our new home in Maryland, on a wide boulevard when we came to a major intersection. I may have had an (undeserved) reputation for going through yellow lights, so the wagon was following fairly closely. When I stopped before the light turned red, it surprised my long-suffering wife, and she crashed into the rear of my newly painted Cougar, and the car top carrier rocketed forward and crashed into the trunk of my car.

Although the crash blocked a six-by-eight lane intersection, fellow drivers seemed more amused than angry. I rushed back to find everyone safe, and son Will helped me unload the carrier to the point where we could drag it to the side of the road.

Sadako vowed she would never drive again, and I did my best to comfort and reassure her, feeling quite noble in not mentioning the damage. We got the cars out of the intersection and found both were completely drivable.

In the process of repacking the gear from the carrier, the kids switched cars and as we drove away, one of the boys said to his mother, "Mom, you should have heard all the bad names Dad called you!" So much for nobility.

Bethesda

Bart Slemmons was the Chief of Orthopedics at Bethesda Naval Hospital, and a good leader. It was an entirely different climate, caring for children, wives, and senior officers.

It seemed that the higher the rank, the more gracious the officer, although unfortunately that often wasn't true of their wives. I bought a large supply of coloring books and crayons for the waiting rooms, and a commander's wife took the whole collection when she left.

At the other end of the spectrum, I found a Marine General calmly sitting alone in the waiting room one noon. It was very unsettling to see a Four Star apparently ignored. When I rushed to help, it turned out he was the Commandant of the Marine Corps, patiently waiting to see Dr. Slemmons. Sometimes there were good people in high places.

Our neighbors were not quite the same as New Englanders, all of whom had been great neighbors. We bought a home in a planned development, in suburban Maryland with a nice community pool for the kids, and a yard that needed work.

Sunset Magazine had an interesting article on how to develop good topsoil using a six-inch covering of sawdust, rototilled into the existing soil.

With the help of a U-Haul 4 x 8 trailer, with added 8-foot-high plywood sides, I found a sawmill nearby, and towed this huge load home. The sawdust was wet, and heavy enough to push the fenders down onto the wheels until another driver alerted me to smoke issuing from burning tires. That was remedied by removing the fenders, not the load.

The landscaping turned out well at the new home, and the children enjoyed the nearby pool and thrived in their new schools. A neighbor, however, came by worried that the sawdust might bring termites. What?

At Bethesda, I was replacing Al Crawford, a colleague who had preceded me in training in Boston. Then he was transferred from Bethesda to San Diego, which had a larger training program. However, in less than two years, he was offered a position as chief of a prestigious civilian training program in Cincinnati. There was no one available immediately to replace me as the pediatric orthopedist at Bethesda, but Dr. Slemmons felt it was more important to have a children's orthopedist at the larger hospital in San Diego, and we were uprooted again, this time somewhat unwillingly, since I had heard that the Naval Hospital in San Diego was a "Zoo."

Our home selection was a bit more deliberate this time, so the family remained in D.C. for three months while I got settled in the billet in San Diego and scouted for houses. By actual count, with a very patient realtor, I inspected 125 homes throughout the county, and by amazing good luck spotted one in Pacific Beach "for sale by owner," with five bedrooms, a generous lot on a hilltop, with a 270-degree view of the city and the ocean, for what was then the steep price of $115,000. Sadako flew out for an inspection, but the choice was obvious to us. The family joined me at Thanksgiving, and we've been here since.

Michael, Suzie, and Willy at the Grand
Canyon, our last cross-country move.

Another transfer, another experience, and a long-suffering wife. Since we were married, we had lived at 19 different addresses, 5 of which were during the last pregnancy. When we got transferred to San Diego, and Sadako found the Japanese markets and Japanese friends, she announced that if I left for another tour, it would be unaccompanied.

In addition to the markets and friends, a new horizon opened for Sadako when some Navy friends introduced her to ceramics. She quickly became quite proficient on the pottery wheel and had access to kilns at NAS Miramar and then on the campus of UCSD. She and a group of other artists formed a group called "Potters by the Dozen." The group started with an annual sale and then expanded to other artist shows. Sadako was an extremely talented and prolific potter with a loyal following. In addition to outfitting our kitchen and providing beautiful decor, she sold most all of her items at special events. She enthusiastically continued her craft for 35 years.

Sadako at the pottery wheel.

Sadako with her creations.

The Orthopedic Department certainly was bigger than anything I had seen, with a 36-bed cast room for orthopedic trauma, and 11 or 12 operating rooms in the third cellar of the "New" Building built on a steep hill. Our offices and clinics at street level were more in tune with the old Balboa Park architecture. The department was made up of staff orthopedists, 12 orthopedic residents, and enlisted medical corps personnel, most of whom were cast technicians, and civilian employees.

When I first arrived, a spirited young cast tech named Kathy McNamara was assigned to work with me. She was a colorful young woman who said she was only willing to work with me because I liked pumpkin ice cream and smoked "Lucky Strike" cigarettes. I eventually was able to quit smoking, but only after shaming myself by bumming cigarettes from my secretary. Kathy became a fast friend for the entire time I was at Balboa, and I was sad to lose track of her when we both eventually left the Navy.

To say she was colorful was a gross understatement. She could hold her own with the biggest and baddest of the male techs. One time, she went to the cast room for something, and one of the techs said, "Kiss my ass." To which she responded, "Bare it." He did, just as the shocked department chief arrived! He was a good churchgoer with a wonderful wife who played the organ.

Kathy also had a "cockapoo" dog which she and her partner, Connie, could no longer keep in their apartment. We inherited "Puddles" and loved her like a family member for some 13 years.

The in-patient facilities occupied much of the "New" Building's nine floors. Occasionally there still were the old-fashioned 8 o'clock personnel inspections in the courtyard of the old hospital.

Most department chiefs had a secretary. The two during my time were both memorable for opposite reasons. The first, whose name mercifully is forgotten, must have gone through a very strange government screening process. She usually yelled from her office to mine, and ordinarily didn't have anything useful to say. The hospital C.O. at the time was named Admiral Rucci. One day she yelled to me, "You've got a call from somebody named Adam Rucci." Such was her grasp of the organization.

The other secretary, Judy Faulwetter, was the absolute best, a 6-foot 2-inch mother of two sons in law enforcement. She had knocked out one of the boys when they sassed her at home. She was a perfect "mother/guardian" and mentor for the staff and residents in the large department and kept me in balance through it all.

We had 12 orthopedic residents in training, with an equal sized staff of surgeons to supervise them in the clinic and the operating rooms. Each staff surgeon spent a month on a trauma team rotation, supervising non-surgical care evaluating new cases with the residents in the 36-bed cast room. During that month they performed no surgery. It was an easy rotation, with a guaranteed departure in time for supper every night. One of the staff orthopedists, with three months of active duty remaining, felt he shouldn't be "wasted" in that rotation, although it was a great opportunity to train the residents.

Each morning began with an x-ray conference, reviewing with the residents all the films taken the day before. This was a good teaching exercise, as well as good quality control for patient care.

After the conferences, the doctor who felt he shouldn't be "wasted" began to appear in my office daily with repetitious arguments why he was too valuable to have to take his turn in the cast room, although the rest of his peers took it in stride.

Finally on a bad morning, he came in with the same old argument, just as I was fielding a call from the Bureau of Medicine about a need for volunteers for temporary overseas duties. With a smile of relief, I said "Nope, you won't have to work in the cast room. You're going to Guam for three months – lots of surgery!" He didn't back-pedal fast enough and spent the last three months of his career on an island with an area of 210 square miles. Some days turn out okay.

As head of pediatric orthopedics, one of the daily activities was an exam of all newborn babies to rule out hip problems. This required me and the residents to invade the newborn nursery, remove the diapers from all 30 to 40 babies and perform the hip exam on little tykes no longer warm and happy. The nurses were not so happy with a ward of squalling babies while we did our work and teaching.

One day, as I was leading the charge and lecturing the residents, we were shocked to hear a loud call from a bed behind a patient's curtain, saying something to the effect of, "Browning, you son of a bitch, come here!"

The residents hushed a bit, fascinated at who could be talking to a Navy Captain like that. Lo and behold, it was Phil's wife Arlene, who had just given birth. She reminded me that I was responsible for the ruination of her white honeymoon nightgowns, and we had a belated laugh.

Southern California Permanente Medical Group

My boss left me to run the department at Balboa when he retired to join SCPMG, the Southern California Permanente Medical Group, or "Kaiser," as it was better known. He urged me to join him there soon, since the time for "vesting" or participating in the Kaiser retirement program required at least 15 years of service before turning age 65.

The work at Balboa was challenging and fun and working with the residents and staff for 7 years was gratifying, but the road ahead held the prospect of becoming an admiral and not a clinical doctor, so I moved to SCPMG in 1982.

There were many gratifying experiences in the clinical realm during 36 years at Kaiser. We took care of disabled kids at five of the "CCS Clinics" in schools throughout the county and developed strong bonds with the kids and their families. Many of these kids with cerebral palsy required muscle surgery, some several times during their childhood.

When I joined, there was not a spine surgeon in SCPMG doing pediatric spine surgery for conditions such as scoliosis (spinal curvature) or congenital spine anomalies and Dr. Randels and I did the cases together. I relished that role, with the help of the finest anesthesiologist I have ever met, Dr. Clyde Jones, from Barbados. He was a man of wisdom, great humor, and a remarkable ability to hypnotize patients with dramatic reduction in their pain levels. After an operation for scoliosis on a young girl, his hypnosis allowed her to be totally free of pain killers for a whole week after surgery.

Perhaps as remarkable was her reaction to the removal of the dressing after a week. Apparently, the removal of tape over an 18" incision was not included in the hypnotic suggestion, and she hit the ceiling when we pulled off the adhesive tape!

Pediatric orthopedics is quite different from adult care. The kids are growing and changing, and often need second or third surgeries. We developed strong bonds with many, many kids and families we cared for.

One memorable young man was born with hand deformities on one side, a congenital amputation of one arm below the elbow on the other, and a discrepancy in leg length projected to be more than seven inches at maturity, as well as an underdeveloped hip joint on the short side. With the help of Dr. John Houkom, a good friend and surgeon with pediatric training, we improved his hip with surgery.

That was followed by a progressive thigh lengthening with a device called the Wagner external fixator, which required four large pins through the skin and the femur, with the bone cut between the two middle pins. The device had a knob on the top which was turned four times daily to lengthen the femur one millimeter at a time, allowing new bone to fill in the gap. The stretch of the skin, muscles, nerves, and vessels was uncomfortable, as might be expected. The boy's father was meticulous about the lengthening, but after he gained the first inch, the four-year-old thought he had had enough and cranked it back down to zero. His father paddled him, cranked it back up to one inch, then added several turns as punishment, and took away the knob. Remarkably the newly forming bone in the gap responded to all these gyrations and still filled in nicely. When the child was older, he had tibial lengthening as well, over his objections, and we were delighted when he finished growing, with less than one inch difference in length of the legs. At maturity, he finally stopped cussing us, reluctantly thanked us and allowed a photo.

Just recently, I received a very welcome call from a 45-year-old woman, on whom we had performed a foot amputation for a congenitally deformed and useless foot, at age four. She was a great patient and quickly resumed karate, kicking with the prosthesis on the involved leg. She reported that she is still fully active with a short leg prosthesis functioning as her foot.

There were many, many patients with simple or complex problems, all of whom were a joy to care for.

"Retirement"

Kaiser has mandatory retirement age at age 65, and for me that was in 2000, after 18 years. The Area Medical Director thought I might help administratively with a problem in our system in Bakersfield, which had no orthopedic department and depended on community surgeons to care for our patients. He suggested that one site visit might be enough and warned me that this would be a short assignment. Eight years later I reminded him I was still working in San Diego and Bakersfield.

Some problems were related to an exclusive contract with a group of eight which allowed charging 140 percent of Medicare rates. Often the reported severity or complexity of cases did not correlate with the service provided. For instance, for a knee injury requiring only diagnostic arthroscopy, there might be billing included for diagnostic arthroscopy, debridement of the joint, ligament repair, and scraping of the kneecap, when only a quick look occurred, with no significant repair.

There were 15 orthopedists in the county. After coffee with each of the surgeons, it was clear that this billing practice was unsustainable. There were several good people eager to work with Kaiser, but they were locked out by the exclusive contract. Only one, Dr. Mark Nystrom, was doing any pediatric work group in his solo practice. He was quite affable and seemed to have avoided clashing with the group.

At the major Catholic Health West Hospitals in Bakersfield, there were only two orthopedic surgeons who would respond to emergency cases, and there was no monthly orthopedic call schedule to support the emergency room physicians at these three major hospitals. This sometimes led to air-lifting a patient to Los Angeles for surgery.

The travel from San Diego to Bakersfield was a big problem, since braving Los Angeles traffic got old quickly and commercial air was no better. A transfer in L.A. was required, which made the trip as time consuming as the drive.

That "aha!" moment arrived when the idea of getting back to flying after a 25-year hiatus seemed worthwhile. A refresher course guided by a great instructor of my age at Palomar Airport near San Diego followed, flying a variety of rental aircraft, and refresher training in instrument flying, which was sometimes humbling.

There was a friendly guy parked on the line with a nice-looking single engine low wing airplane called a "Diamond Star." The plane was made of composite materials which were much more aerodynamic than riveted metal.

After I tried various airplane rentals for a while, he got me to buy a Diamond Star for the frequent trips to Bakersfield, which worked out much better in terms of dependability and availability.

There is a mountain pass called "the Grapevine" on the main highway between Los Angeles and the Central Valley which tended to collect bad weather and icing at night particularly. The Diamond Star handled these problems well, since the airplane was able to get up to 14,000 to 15,000 feet, readily, and had good instrument capability. The only anxiety factor involved the possibility of an engine failure over the mountains, at night, with no airports within gliding range.

A pediatric colleague, Scott Shoemaker, joined me for the clinics in Bakersfield. Shortly after 9/11, with heightened armed security at airports, when we arrived after dark one night, we had to climb the fence to get to our rental car, hoping we wouldn't be spotted by the sentries!

Scott was an excellent co-pilot, and showed great promise as a pilot, quickly acquiring take-off and landing skills. On one occasion he helped avoid disaster when he noted a failure of the fuel tank selector crank before I did. The inability to switch tanks in flight led to a "squeaker" with a night landing and only four gallons of fuel remaining. The maintenance folks found it was a failed $7.95 roller pin which connected the fuel selector to the right- and left-wing tanks. Ours was the first case ever reported, and it led to an inspection of all DA-40s in the world.

Twin Star.

Anticipating a long-term commitment in Bakersfield, I became interested in a twin-engine Diamond aircraft called the Twin Star, with high altitude capability, a "glass cockpit," a great navigation panel, and another unique feature – diesel engines. The Austrian company modified Mercedes engines for light planes, resulting in a very dependable engine.

Bill, George, and Sadako on a post-
retirement trip across the country.

That power plant also offered great advantages in economy. Translating fuel consumption from gallons per hour to miles per gallon, it got better mileage than my Toyota van. It flew and climbed nicely on one engine, with a service ceiling of nearly 25,000 feet!

Dr. Amir Amirpour

We met one sainted man, an orthopedist from Iran, who became a good friend. He had escaped when the Revolution occurred, did his orthopedic training in London, and was fully qualified. He was not eligible to sit for the exams to become a Fellow of the American Academy of Orthopedic Surgery (AAOS) since his training had to be in the U.S. or Canada to qualify.

He and one or two others in the county were the only ones who responded to pleas for help from the Bakersfield E.R. doctors. The group which controlled the hospital board had decreed that it was necessary to be a Fellow of the AAOS to have surgical privileges, thus preventing him from operating in the Catholic Health West hospitals. That travesty persisted until it was discovered that the chairman of the group had been unable to pass the boards.

After my off-hand suggestion that the situation might be an interesting article for the local newspaper, the obstacles seemed to melt away, and Dr. Amirpour was able to continue his work more effectively. He and his delightful wife continued to be good friends and counselors for the entire time I was there.

Management

When I arrived in Bakersfield in 1980, the Area Medical Director, Bill Geckler, a psychiatrist, was a good counselor regarding community politics, and very helpful in getting me started. When he retired he was replaced by a female physician, who did not favor me much for reasons unknown, despite my good rapport with the Kaiser pediatricians, most community colleagues, our administrators, and the hospitals.

We were urged to start a pediatric orthopedic clinic soon after arrival, and people and resources were made available, including a wonderful young man named DaShawn Warren, a cast technician who was great with kids, staff, and colleagues. The nurses were also outstanding, and rapidly adapted to new concepts of orthopedic care for kids. There was also excellent radiology support, which eventually led to the formation of a spine clinic.

Since I had surgical privileges at all three Catholic Health West Hospitals, it was necessary to respond to emergency cases for Kaiser orthopedic patients at all three, a stretch until we were able to hire more orthopedists.

With the encouragement of Dr. Mark Nystrom, a recruiting process began. He joined us full time and recruited one of the guys from the eight-man group to join us. One hand surgeon, Dr. Matt Mallerich, joined us for clinics and surgery and was a great asset, although he was at a point in his career when it wasn't practical for him to become a full time Kaiser doctor.

Kaiser recruiting also found a promising candidate for us, a hand surgeon in Florida who was willing to move. She was a charming young woman, and probably the first black surgeon in Kern County. Her husband made arrangements to sell their house in Florida while they looked for homes in Bakersfield.

Some of the male surgeons were not delighted to see a black woman operating at the "their hospitals," and mounted an attack on her, asserting that she was "slow" in the O.R., although the quality of her work was impeccable.

This led to a regrettable situation when the Area Medical Director suddenly ordered me to fire her immediately on a Friday during clinic and sent a physician monitor and a security person to make sure she did not contact her husband for help or support. In retrospect, I should have resigned rather than comply.

After this unfortunate occurrence, it was obvious that my further efforts would not be supported. Our four orthopedists with superb staff no longer needed my help although some of the complex pediatric needs were still a problem. It was time to return to San Diego for another eight years of clinical and administrative roles at three different offices.

Post-Bakersfield Flying

After the Bakersfield trips ended in 2008, another flying opportunity quickly replaced that. There is a volunteer organization called "Angel Flight" in Los Angeles which coordinates requests for air transport of medical patients from all over the West to the major hospitals in San Diego, Los Angeles, and San Francisco.

That was a wonderful opportunity to spend time and money flying for a purpose, rather than just boring holes in the sky. The opportunities to help extended from Calexico to the northern border of California and included meeting many charming and interesting people.

A family trip to Boeing Field in Seattle was memorable for a quite different reason. After landing in Seattle, something cut one of the tires just as we taxied off the runway and were directed into a slot between two giant Gulfstream planes. The Base Operator wanted me to move to a light airplane parking slot, but we quickly found that neither towing or trying to taxi at full power would budge the Twin Star. It was a Friday, and there were no tires for this aircraft in the Seattle area. The only possible replacement was at a Diamond facility in Vancouver, and we didn't have passports.

After an urgent call to my great friend Henry Sickels, the manager at our home base in San Diego, he worked miracles and was able to find a tire in Houston and have it delivered by 9:00am Monday. The Base Operator in Seattle was placated, allowing for a nice weekend visit with friends and family, and an uneventful flight back home on Monday afternoon.

On another cross-country flight, as Sadako and I were flying north over Dana Point near Long Beach, there was a sudden power loss on the left engine, and she commented, "That propeller looks funny." All instrument readings were normal except for the low RPM on the left, so L.A. center cleared us back to Montgomery Field in San Diego.

With the errant engine feathered, the airplane flew normally, on a route over airfields at Camp Pendleton, Oceanside, Palomar, MCAS Miramar, with an uneventful landing at Montgomery. The airplane flew quite nicely on a single engine, but once off the runway it wouldn't taxi worth a darn, and we had to be towed back to the maintenance hangar.

They found a hydraulic pump had failed, shedding metal shavings which clogged the hydraulic propeller pitch control. After the diagnosis, new parts quickly fixed the problem.

Medical work at Kaiser continued until COVID days, and we also had time for memorable flights, the longest of which was from San Diego to Las Vegas, New Mexico, Twin Cities, Chicago, and then on to Washington D.C. to pick up George, my college roommate. He flew with us to Pensacola to relive old memories and see the spectacular Naval Aviation Museum.

Then he headed back to D.C. and Sadako and I flew west along the southern route. Many nice people helped us at the large and small airports along the way, even offering vehicles and lodging suggestions for the night.

Weddings

I had been a long-time attendee at All Souls Church in Point Loma, where two of our kids were married under quite different circumstances. Our daughter Suzie was married to Todd Lincoln, in a memorable wedding, complete with a (rented) Bentley for the day, a huge reception at the Sheraton on Harbor Island, and my niece, Jennifer Hinshaw, singing parts of the service.

Son Will and Marie Johnson were also married there. However, Marie's mother opposed all religious ceremonies, and their marriage was scheduled to be a civil ceremony by Bob Stahl, a judge who lived next door, at the Sheraton Torrey Pines.

We wanted a "real" wedding as well and our favorite minister, David Heaney, who also married Suzie and Todd agreed to a family-only wedding at the All Souls Episcopal Church chapel after 3:00 p.m. on Good Friday afternoon. He was the most inspirational minister I ever met.

Marty

I continued to attend All Souls and met Marty Engler, who was one of the regulars at coffee hour after the early service. He was very modest but eventually we found out that he had been a fighter pilot during WWII, got shot down in France, and was rescued by the Tank Corps. He wrote an engaging book called "Foxhunt 24" about those adventures.

Marty had been an executive with San Diego Gas and Electric Company and in addition to being the lead engineer on the major gas pipeline running through Southern California, he worked to develop the company's liquified natural gas (LNG) program. He and his wife moved to Texas where he continued in the LNG industry and then settled in El Paso. After retiring, he studied for and completed his Airframe and Powerplant Mechanic (A&P) license. His happy retirement years in Texas were spent restoring and flying four vintage airplanes. After his wife passed away, he returned to San Diego to be with his daughter Kate.

A backyard visit with Marty.

I was still flying the Twin Star and invited him along; there began a friendship of many years, flying together from 2012 to 2018. There are many small airports in odd places throughout Southern California, some with nice restaurants. I think Marty and I visited most of them, from Tehachapi to Big Bear to French Valley near Temecula, among many others. Marty's favorite was French Valley, which had a good restaurant, but I think what made it his favorite was the chocolate sundae he always ordered for dessert with extra whipped cream and a cherry to top it off!

Despite his modesty, he was still quite capable in the cockpit. After a good lunch at Big Bear, though, in the warm afternoon sun, he preferred to doze, and leave it to me to get us home. He and his wife are together now at Fort Rosecrans National Cemetery at the tip of Point Loma. And leave it to him to ensure his burial site had an excellent view of the runway at NAS North Island.

The End of Flying

Between the pesky FAA and their demands for ever more medical reports at renewal time each year, and the annual liability insurance coverage escalating to $10,000 per year, by 2018 it was time to quit. I look back at a total of 4000 hours pilot time, with 900 hours in the Twin Star, and so many great memories of my flying adventures!

Postscript

My wife and I have three amazing children (is there any other kind?) who settled happily in San Diego when the Navy transferred us out here. There were a million adventures involving the kids, but the following is one reminder of why we're all still smiling. Son Will and his mother were always at odds over the peanut butter. She insisted it had to be refrigerated; he wanted it soft and spreadable. After a long back and forth, one morning we found the jar on the kitchen counter glued securely to a large 2 x 6 plank!

Will, Bill, Sadako, Suzie, and Michael.